PLANNING SCHOOLS FOR USE OF AUDIO-VISUAL MATERIALS

NO. 3
THE AUDIO-VISUAL INSTRUCTIONAL MATERIALS CENTER

January 1954

DEPARTMENT OF AUDIO-VISUAL INSTRUCTION

NATIONAL EDUCATION ASSOCIATION

1201 Sixteenth Street, N.W., Washington, D. C.

PRICE: $1.00

BUILDINGS AND EQUIPMENT COMMITTEE
Department of Audio-Visual Instruction

Co-Chairmen — Irene F. Cypher and A. J. Foy Cross

Thomas E. Batson	H. E. Hansen	Don Newcomer
David Bernhardt	Alexander H. Howard, Jr.	R. A. Petrie
Kenneth L. Bowers	Charles E. Luminati	L. A. Pinkney
Maurice Camp	D. F. Lyman	V. Harry Rhodes
Lloyd J. Cartwright	Lillian E. McNulty	R. H. Shreve
J. Wesley Crum	Russell Meinhold	Don White
Raymond Denno	Herman M. Myhrman	Harvey J. Woltman

VISUALS

Illustrations included in the handbook were obtained thru the courtesy of:

Alexis I. Dupont Special School District, Wilmington, Del. 2a, 5a, 15, 18, 77

Arlington County Schools, Va. 24, 31, 64

Baltimore City Schools, Md. 28c, 33

Barnett and Jaffee 54

Thomas E. Batson, Washington, D.C., Public Schools - Preparing architectural materials for reproduction.

Brumberger 39, 53

Calif. State Department of Education 29b, 49, 56, 58

Central Washington College, Office of Visual Education 22, 62

Charlotte City Schools, N.C. 32

W. D. Clapp Company 66a

Jack C. Coffey Company 40, 66b

Conn. State Department of Education 20

Dade County Schools, Fla. 6c, 12, 28d, 29a

Davidson County Schools, Tenn. 44, 50

Eastman Kodak Company, 34a, 73, 74b

Fiberbilt Case Company 30

Fulton County Schools, Ga. 6a, 8, 27, 28b, 43, 55, 59, 61, 75

Hammond City Schools, Ind. 17

Kanawha County Schools, W.Va. 10, 14

Louisville City Schools, Ky. 16

Alan Mogenson, Work Simplification Conference, N.Y. 36

Neumade Products Corporation 34b&c, 35, 37, 41, 42, 51, 74a

New Albany City Schools, Ind. 68, 69

N. J. State Department of Education 71, 72

N. Y. Telephone Company 76

N. Y. University, School of Education 1, 3, 4, 19, 70

Oak Ridge City Schools, Tenn. 5b, 7, 63, 67

Remington Rand, Inc. 52, 57, 60, 78, 79

Alta Robinson, State College of Washington 21

Rochester City Schools, N.Y. 2b, 9, 28a, 65

Margaret Rufsvold and Paul Seagers, Indiana University 23

St. Louis City Schools, Mo. 13, 26

Salem City Schools, Oreg. 6b

San Diego County Schools, Calif. 25

Wallach and Associates 38, 45, 46, 47, 48

Young America Films, Inc. Cover Cartoon

ACKNOWLEDGEMENTS

Appreciation is due the many persons and organizations that assisted in the preparation and review of the manuscript. Special thanks are due the representatives of the American Institute of Architects, the American Association of School Administrators, the American Library Association, the Association of Chief State School Audio-Visual Officers, and the many members of the Department of Audio-Visual Instruction who assisted with the publication.

CONTENTS

Foreword 4

The IM Center 5
    What a Center Is 5
    What a Center Is Not 7
    Service Depends on Leadership 8
    Respective Roles of School and School System Centers 9
    Organizational Patterns 12
    Services To Be Provided by an AV-IM Center 14
    Summary 24

Housing Basic Functions 25
    Space Needs 32
        Storage, Handling, Repair, and Distribution of Materials 32
        Storage, Handling, Care, and Distribution of Equipment 50
        Production of Materials 54
        Preview and Auditioning 58
        Administration 60
    Summary 61

Achieving Goals 62

Appendix

    Bibliography 64

    Brief list of companies manufacturing and/or distributing
    equipment for IM Centers 69

    What is Your School's IM Quotient? 77

FOREWORD

In these days of compulsory education laws and chronological promotion, when the spread of pupil ability and interest in each classroom becomes ever wider, it is important that the teacher and the students have access to many types of aids to make the classroom an interesting and profitable place for young people. Even if it were desirable, it is no longer possible for a teacher to carry on the textbook type of instruction which was universal a half-century ago. That was suited to a system of mass education in which the atypical pupil usually dropped out of school at an early age. Today the school attempts to meet the needs of all the children with their wide range of abilities and interests. The teacher has to use all the laws of learning and the means of stimulating learning activities if he is to meet the challenge of the modern classroom.

It is for this reason that the idea for instructional material centers is spreading rapidly thruout the school systems of this country. Such a department is specifically designed to bring to the attention and to the repertoire of the teacher the greatest possible variety of instructional materials.

The reader will find this manual simple but complete; practical yet forward-looking. It builds up in very convincing fashion the ideal of service which is the fundamental philosophy of an instructional materials center.

The manual presents very clearly and in considerable detail the part that good leadership plays in making the center effective in the life of teachers and students. It is this human factor which is so often overlooked in treatises on administration, supervision, or instruction. No matter how well-planned a line-and-staff organization may be, no matter how many dollars are spent in the school budget for materials and equipment, the factor that will make or break the effectiveness of any department in a school system is the human factor.

This manual will help you establish, operate, and make successful an instructional materials center in your school system. It is well worth all the study you can give it.

Amo De Bernardis
Assistant Superintendent
Portland, Oregon, Public Schools

THE IM CENTER

What A Center Is

The instructional materials center is a service agency. Its chief purpose, and its only justification for existence, is to provide good learning experiences for pupils and adults of the community. It is a resource center for teaching tools, materials, and ideas. The personnel and all the materials and other resources made available thru the center must be devoted to the improvement of learning experiences. The housing of the staff and resources of such a center, either in an individual school or in a city or county school system, is the subject of this brochure.

1. The audio-visual instructional materials center is a service agency.

Parents and educators generally agree that schools must constantly be improved if young people are to be adequately prepared to meet the demands of the modern world. They also agree that youth's classroom education can be greatly enriched by bringing the world to him thru planned audio-visual experiences (5:89-96). Unfortunately not all who are concerned with education understand that *the design and equipment of the school building itself must change to meet these demands for a new and better school-community educational program.*

One of the ways in which schools are adapting to changes in methods and purposes of education is thru the development of instructional materials centers. The center is more than just space, materials, and equipment. It is a well-planned, flexible space housing carefully chosen materials and equipment, and serviced by effective professional people dedicated to a program of the best possible education for the young people and adults of the community.

The center contains carefully chosen instructional materials of many types. In fact, the scope of the resources available thru such a center should be limited only by the needs of those who make use of it.

2. Many types of instructional materials should be available for pupil-teacher use

There may be cataloged in such a center all the books, pamphlets, clippings, magazines, films, filmstrips, slides, maps, globes, flat pictures, community-resources files, microfilms, stereoscopic materials, museum materials, records and transcriptions, radio and television files, and any other resources which may assist in the instructional and learning jobs to be done. It is a place, too, in which new and different instructional materials are planned, produced, and experimentally tested and evaluated. It can also serve as a clearinghouse for inter-library loans between schools and between the school and various organizations, such as film libraries, public and private libraries, museums, and local, regional, state, and national agencies.

What A Center Is Not

The center is not, as erroneously supposed by some school planners, a classroom selected by some mysterious process and designated as the room to which all classes desiring to see pictures are assigned. Such rooms are a hindrance to the school program and have been condemned by modern educators.

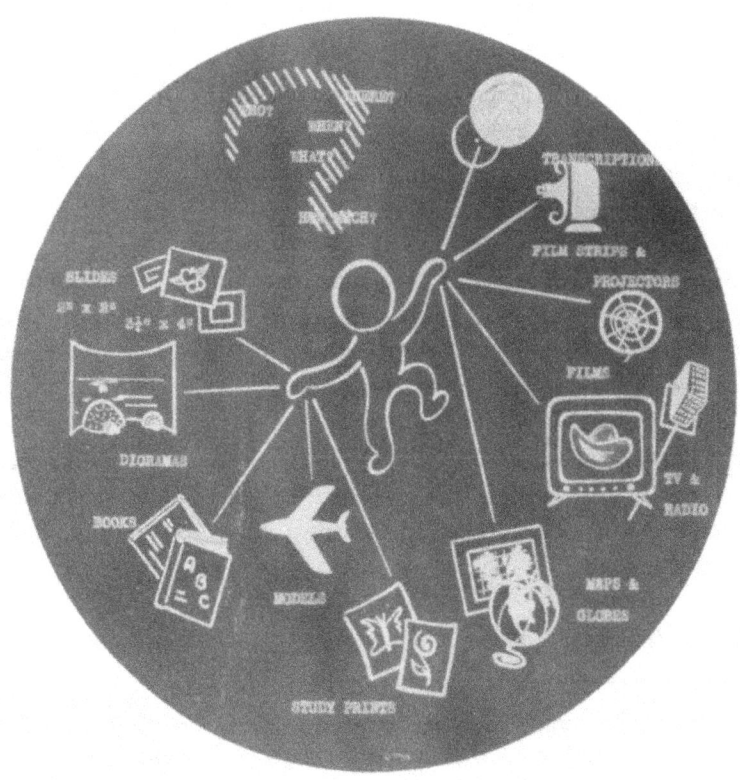

3. The materials center provides a wide range of instructional materials.

Neither is the center merely a place where films are obtained and showings scheduled. While the center assists the classroom teacher in making optimum use of motion pictures, it is not a motion picture centered operation.

Service Depends On Leadership

The nature of a center and the service it will render is affected by the leadership and ability of the person who directs it and the amount of time the administration allows for performance of the duties of this office. The director's or coordinator's[1] dynamic interest in assisting the cause of good learning is expressed in a very real kind of professional leadership.

He makes the most of every opportunity to enhance the creative abilities and skills of classroom teachers by securing the ready accessibility of a rich supply of carefully selected instructional materials.

He is an expediter, a cutter of the red tape and routine which might otherwise stand in the way of wide and wise use of instructional materials.

He is familiar with desirable utilization technics.

He is alert to the possibilities for service to the instructional program of the school and community.

He knows the nature of the contributions which might be anticipated from a well conducted field trip, from the proper use of reference books, from the projection of flat pictures, from the use of filmstrips, or from the construction of lantern slides.

He knows the purposes of the various steps in approaching, identifying, analyzing, and solving the problems in a unit of learning. He knows where and how and which aids to learning might be used in connection with such units.

Upon this key person is bestowed at once the opportunity and

---

[1] In this brochure, the term "director" is used to designate the person in a school system who is responsible for the audio-visual program. The term "coordinator" or "building coordinator" is used to refer to the person responsible for the audio-visual program within a single school.

responsibility of assisting boys, girls, teachers, and others of his community in the proper use of the many learning opportunities at their disposal.

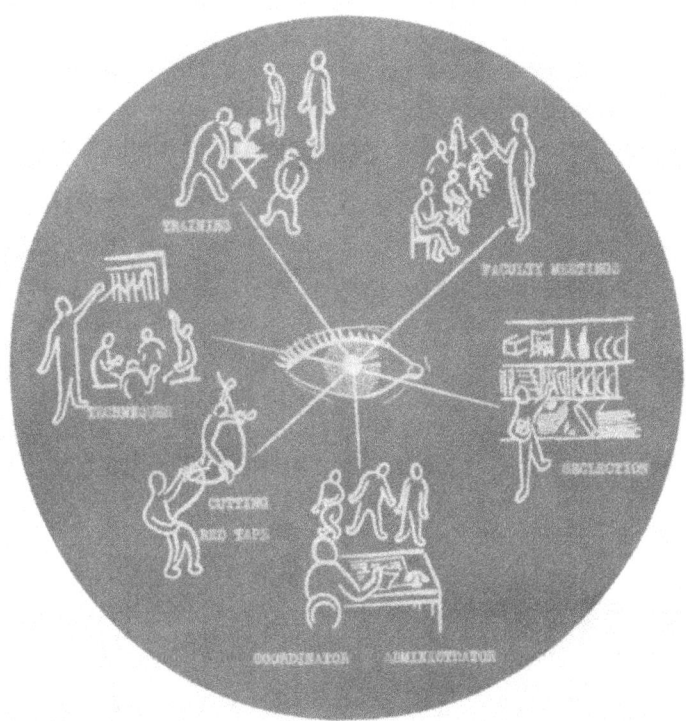

4. The coordinator or director of a materials center plays a key role in setting the learning environment.

Even a skilled leader cannot adequately fulfil his responsibilities unless the other school leaders are also sufficiently interested in providing the best learning environment for students. The administration must provide *sufficient personnel with sufficient time* to carry out the objectives of an instructional materials program. The administration must see that the instructional materials center, its materials, and its personnel are *advantageously housed*.

Respective Roles of School and School System Centers

The normal place for the actual utilization of most audio-visual and other instructional materials is the classroom itself, under the guidance and with the help of the classroom teacher. The center, however, plays an important supporting role. The importance of the center and the degree of its importance to the instructional program is measured by its usefulness as a source of advice and service.

Altho instructional materials should be as accessible as possible to the teacher and the pupils, it is neither possible nor practical for any one teacher to amass and catalog, or keep readily available, a private collection of all materials and other instructional resources necessary to the modern classroom. Properly conceived, the instructional materials center in a school becomes a place to which all teachers may turn for help in discovering, obtaining, and using instructional materials and other resources, as well as any equipment essential to the use of the materials.

5. All schools should have collections of materials such as mounted pictures and maps.

The most important instructional materials services should be provided in the individual school. Limitation of available funds, however, makes this goal unachievable for all but a few communities. For example, most individual schools cannot build up an adequate film or professional library. On the other hand, it is usually possible for an individual school to have a basic collection of filmstrips, slides, recordings, maps, charts, and other materials and equipment which are relatively inexpensive and frequently used.

Experience has shown that, *when the individual school cannot satisfy all needs, a central materials center serving a group of schools is the most satisfactory answer* (19, 34, 75, 77). Usually these central materials centers serve city or county school systems. They provide all schools in their service area with a wider range of instructional materials than can be afforded by an individual school and make possible efficient and economical programs of improved utilization of instructional materials.

6. Central materials centers serve city or county systems.

The degree of centralization of materials and facilities is a matter to be decided by a local school system. A balance must be achieved between the ideal of complete decentralization and the practicalities of a situation. Certain basic instructional services must be housed in the individual school, no matter how small the school. However, many services may be housed in either individual schools or in the school system center. The decision, naturally, affects the housing needs.

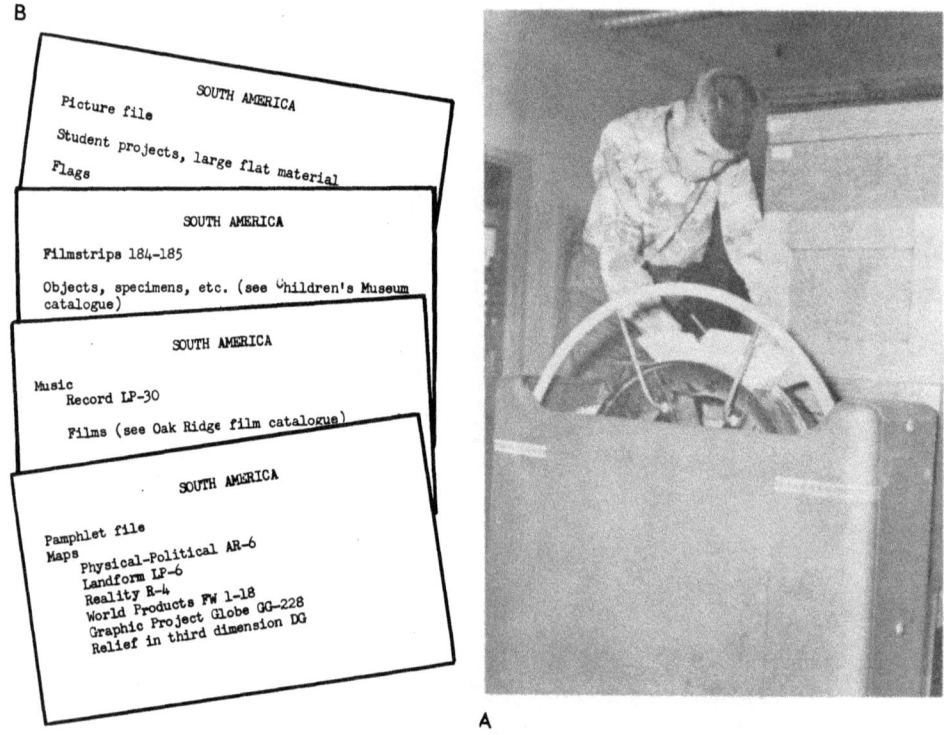

7. On this wheel card file the student will find references to many kinds of appropriate learning materials.

Organizational Patterns

No learning will be quite complete until all the materials and resources *of the school* itself have been scanned for possible usefulness. No learning experience can reach optimum effectiveness until all the resources *of the community* — its people and places, its things and activities, its surroundings, its organizations, and its patterns and processes — have been brought to bear upon it. No learning experience will be fully rounded unless the source lists, catalogs, and other indexes to resources *outside the community* have been studied for possible help.

The management and flow of all these resources to the learning situation and help in using them are the jobs of the instructional materials coordinator and director.

The administrative pattern which will serve best to enable a school or school system to achieve the ideal teaching-learning situation described above will vary from locality to locality. An important determinant is the administrative pattern of the school system. It is essential that the director of an instructional materials center work closely with those persons and groups developing and improving curriculums.

Normally, it is essential that educators specially qualified and trained in the field of instructional materials be appointed as directors and building coordinators of instructional materials programs. It is important that a director's professional background include curriculum development and specialized training in the selection, organization, administration, and use of all types of instructional materials.[2] Except in schools having very few teachers, this administrator should devote full time to leadership, inservice education, curriculum development, and the general administration of the instructional materials program.

The purpose of any such organization of personnel and services is *to bring to the teacher and his pupils the materials and resources which they need to develop the very best possible educational program for themselves* (3:183-218). There are working examples of this goal being met in schools where library materials and nonbook, audio-visual, materials are housed separately and have individual program directors working cooperatively. There are also working examples of this goal being met in schools where the book and audio-visual materials and equipment are combined in one instructional materials center.

Under either administrative plan, or combinations thereof, all materials available to all teachers should be cataloged in the school and school system libraries. Such a comprehensive file helps teachers and students to find appropriate instructional materials (51:56). Much of this instructional material will not be found in the library or in the audio-visual instructional materials center but in classrooms or in the community.

---

[2] A suggested pattern of requirements for the preparation of audio-visual directors was developed by the Professional Education Committee of the Department of Audio-Visual Instruction at the National Conference in 1952. A report is included in *DAVI Boston Conference Proceedings 1952* (22).

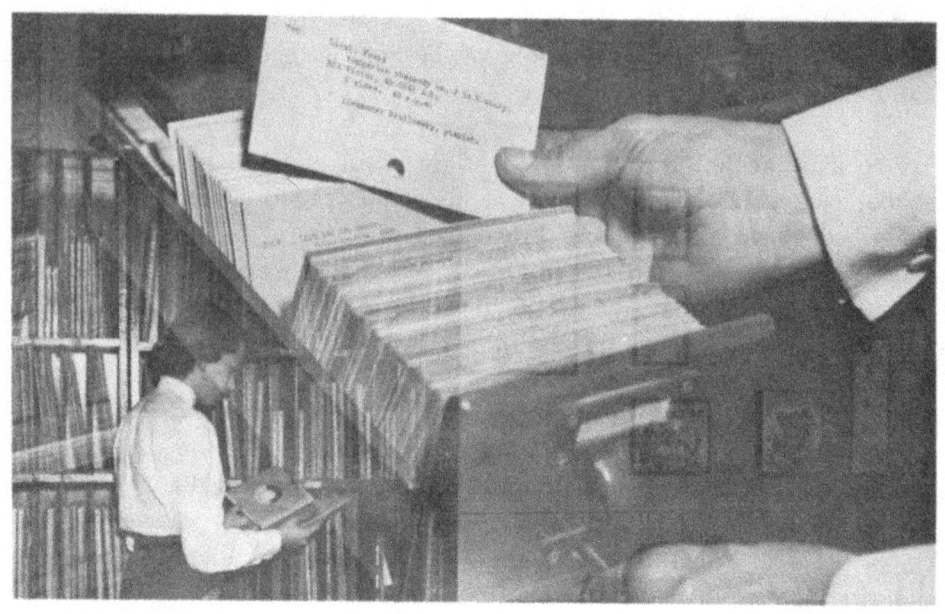

8. The filing of catalog cards for all instructional materials in one card catalog facilitates use.

The purpose of a centralized card file is to give the location and pertinent information concerning the availability of all kinds of teaching materials. For example, a vacuum pump or a model of a heart may well be kept in the room where it is used most frequently and yet may be made readily accessible to others thru its identification in the center's file. Likewise, a privately owned slide collection of Mexican scenes might be identified as available from a lay member of the community.

Obviously the facilities for housing the instructional materials center must be tailored to meet local needs. Regardless of the administrative pattern under which these services are made available, certain building-space requirements must be provided. These are discussed in the second part of this brochure.

Services To Be Provided by an AV-IM Center

The persons officially responsible for the AV instructional materials center will be called upon to render such learning-aid services as:

1. Stimulating and helping teachers, pupils, and others to make the most of instructional resources
2. Serving as a resource person for curriculum planning councils and other committees

3. Cataloging and organizing materials for use
4. Providing for cooperative exchange of services and materials
5. Assisting in formal and informal inservice education
6. Assisting in the use of instructional equipment
7. Providing mechanical and clerical services
8. Producing simple teaching materials.

9. Every school needs a corps of trained student assistants.

The building coordinator, or the center director, who tries to do all these tasks alone is likely to become so overburdened as to become quite ineffective. These tasks are joint enterprises where the coordinator provides stimulation and help but the teachers and students assume the major responsibility for the proper use of instructional materials and opportunities.

The services listed above may be provided thru the school or school system center but will usually be provided to some degree by both. At the present time in most localities, the emphasis will be upon centers serving groups of schools. In some rural communities, however, the central or consolidated school is a unit in itself.

The director of a school system materials center will have emphases in his service program different from those of building coordinators working in cooperation with him. The building coordinator is in closer contact with classroom activities. The director performs many of his services with or thru the building coordinators.

The director of a center works more frequently with curriculum planning councils and other citywide or countywide committees. The building coordinator serves more often as an implementer and interpreter of curriculum needs, assisting school or subject area committees and individual teachers.

The administrative responsibilities of a director are naturally greater than those of a building coordinator. Problems of selection of materials and equipment for purchase, booking of materials housed in the central materials center, transportation of materials from school to school, and budget require more of the time of the director of a citywide or countywide center.

Stimulating and helping teachers, pupils, and others to make the most of instructional resources — If the center and its resources are to be used to the greatest advantage, the coordinator should see to it that materials and services go to the learning situation whenever possible. Too much emphasis on centralized storage, control, maintenance, and circulation may stifle availability of learning resources. Taking services *to* the classroom may involve the voluntary offering of materials directly to teachers and others who need the facilities of the center.

Service will not end here. The coordinator must be ready to suggest better items to use, or to help in deciding which of several may be most valuable. He may make major contributions to the class during the selection process by organizing the production of the necessary materials as part of the activity of the class group, or by helping to get pupils and teachers out into the community in search of valuable experiences.

The instructional materials coordinator will realize that there is no fixed method or technic for using instructional materials and other resources. Good teachers, working with other teachers, sharing experiences, combining plans and ideas, will be a most fruitful source of stimulating more and better use of good materials. When such cooperative procedure is not possible, the coordinator may serve as the go-between for this useful technic. One of the greatest sources of ideas and rich learning experience lies in the pupils themselves and in interested people from outside the school.

10. Teachers in a county center making erasable maps and globes.

The effective coordinator will stimulate and assist in experimental tryout and evaluation of materials and learning procedures. He will make every effort to have groups of teachers, pupils, and others participate in such evaluation.

The coordinator must become familiar with many instructional and learning technics and combinations and variations of technics. An otherwise routine school experience may take on new life thru the use or a new book, a field trip, a new picture, a map or graph, or a resource person, used at just the right time. Setting up a corner for a working group, providing construction materials and advice, guiding a student committee into a new research area, or providing sources for individual search or study might be the move which would bring inspiration into a learning experience.

Serving as a resource person for curriculum planning councils and other committees — The personnel of the center should be well prepared and readily available to assist curriculum planners in selecting and adapting instructional materials and other learning resources. Frequently such service will require that the center have on hand and ready for use such items as lists of materials, teacher's guides and manuals, outlines of resource units, sample picture sets, pamphlets, professional books, exhibits and displays, slide sets, and production outlines.

11. A curriculum committee cannot work effectively under such adverse conditions.

The coordinator of the center should also be prepared to serve as a resource in aiding producers in preparing worthwhile educational materials. He should know what materials are needed and essential, and the educational standards which such materials should meet.

Cataloging and organizing materials for use — It is essential that cataloging and organizing instructional materials facilitate the use of the collection and make it more readily available. It must be emphasized that system is necessary or utilization will fail. On the other hand, a preoccupation with the collecting, storing, and cataloging services must be warned against or the full potential of use may never be fully realized. As time savers, special attention should be accorded commercial aids as opposed to homemade systems in establishing the records for the organization of materials (50:55-68).

The developing single card file system of instructional materials found in many local and county centers is worthy of attention. "Very briefly described, the single card file provides ready reference to available instructional materials of all sorts. For example, teachers in an individual school building, or a city or county school system, get together and explore their resources and make a preliminary inventory of all available instructional-experience resources in their area. The tentative inventory when completed will be a descriptive list of all films, slides, reference books, maps, excursion points, resource persons, collections, models, demonstration apparatus, etc., which are the property or are other-

12. Films are racked according to Dewey Decimal System. The shelving is of wood. Plastic labels are stapled to the shelves to indicate the proper location of each film. Lettering on plastic can be removed with cleaner fluid and can be replaced with a pen.

wise available to teachers and pupils and other interested members of the community. The list will show individually owned teacher or pupil or parent collections of pictures or slides or apparatus and similar materials as well as that which is community property. Once listed, all these resources are individually described and cataloged on library cards of various colors. A different color card is used for each category of material. The films, for example, are described and cataloged on blue cards, the reference books on white, the maps on yellow, and so on. Altogether the blues, the whites, and all other cards, all type-categories are arranged under interest-area headings in a single card file system. Then in making use of the file the persons needing instructional aid, a visual aid, perhaps, on apple growing will consult the file system with particular attention to the interest area labeled "FRUITS" or possibly "FRUIT GROWING and PROCESSING." In this section of the file the investigator will find an array of cards of various colors. Thumbing through the blue ones he will read descriptions of available films on fruits; the white cards will show him the reference books on his problem, etc. Each card shows clearly where and how the resource which it represents may be obtained.

```
┌─────────────────────────────────────────────────────────────────┐
│  BLUE              INTEREST AREA              FILM              │
│                                               S  Si  C  B&W     │
│                                         NO. REELS        TIME   │
│  TITLE:                                                         │
│                                                                 │
│  DESCRIPTION:                                                   │
│                                                                 │
│  AVAILABILITY:  WHERE?                        COST              │
│                                                                 │
│  HOW?                                                           │
│                                                                 │
│  LEARNING RESOURCES FILE                                        │
│  WENACTIMA PUBLIC SCHOOLS                                       │
└─────────────────────────────────────────────────────────────────┘
```

"Illustration of card used in single card-file system of cataloging instructional materials. Card shown is blue in color and is used for 16 mm films only. Note that card is marked BLUE in upper left corner to facilitate use by persons who are not color sensitive. Cards describing other types of materials are of different colors, (e.g. maps on yellow cards, reference books on white cards, etc.)" (16:42-43).

Providing for cooperative exchange of services and materials — There is a need for cooperative exchange between a building center and other sources of instructional materials, including the systemwide centers in larger communities. At times, persons of particular skill in construction activities, in organizing dramatic activity, in leading groups thru various field experiences may be "borrowed" from another building or school, or may be found among the nonschool members of the community.

Some much needed materials are so rare, so expensive, or so bulky that they are available on a loan basis only. To enrich the whole school

13. Unit collections ready for distribution from a large city center.

program the instructional materials center can seek out such resources and make them available in the classroom. Likewise, thru cooperative arrangements with other agencies, the instructional materials coordinator can make local resources available to persons outside the local school or community.

Assisting in formal and informal inservice education — It is difficult to conceive of a situation which is likely to arise in any inservice pattern where the instructional materials coordinator cannot be of assistance. A coordinator should be especially alert to insure that opportunies for experience with materials which fill important instructional needs are included in the inservice training program of the school.

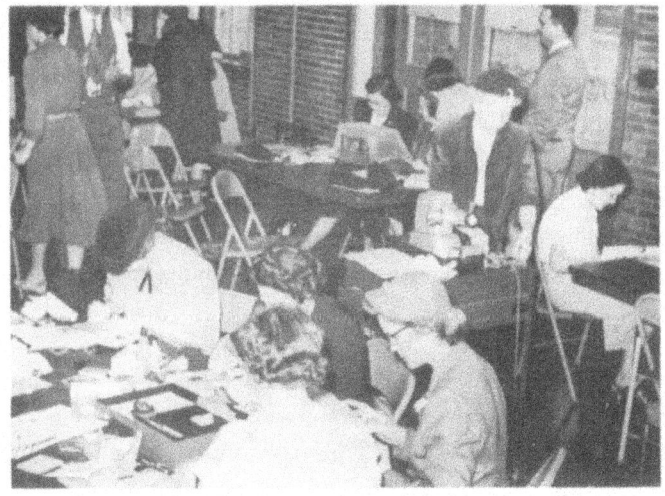

14. Teachers in a materials workshop making slides for classroom use.

Assisting in the use of instructional equipment — The purchase, maintenance, and use of certain equipment, such as projectors and record players, should be administered thru the instructional materials center. Building coordinators are usually responsible for the training and organization of a corps of equipment operators.

A maximum of good use of such equipment is much more likely when the responsibility for its suitability, its effective scheduling, its correct operation, and its proper maintenance is placed in the hands of a well prepared instructional materials coordinator. In most schools and school systems, only minor repairs and simple maintenance operations are performed in the center. Overhauling and major repairs are contracted to accredited service people in the community.

15. Members of the student projection corps practice the threading of a motion picture projector.

Equipment is sometimes of little value to anyone because no one in the building has assumed the responsibility for its good use and upkeep. On the other hand, such equipment is of little value if it is placed under the guardianship of persons whose chief purpose is to take care of school property.

Providing mechanical and clerical services — Effective class activity depends upon a minimum of interruptions and on a concentration of effort upon immediate ends. The classroom teacher should not be

16. Booking requests for materials by telephone. These files hold booking cards for 2075 motion pictures, 1850 filmstrips, and 100 pieces of equipment.

bothered with details of supply, records or maintenance of materials and equipment. Furthermore, routine operation should be so simple as to free as much as possible of the coordinator's time for personal attention to the teaching and learning problems of the school and other community agencies.

The arrangement and equipment of the building center must give all teachers easy access to the catalog files and to all cataloged material in the building center. This service should be as nearly as possible on a "self-serve" basis. This "self-serve" routine should provide for checking out and returning material and equipment so that accounts may be kept straight.

Producing simple teaching materials — Some of the most valuable teaching materials are those simple ones which are produced locally by teachers and/or pupils to meet a specific need. Some common examples are posters, bulletin board displays, models, felt boards, handmade slides, and tape recordings. Building coordinators should provide advice and assistance in the mounting of pictures, with simple lettering and coloring technics, and the use of many kinds of construction materials.

17. A student books equipment for classroom use.

The director of a school system center will be called upon to supervise more complex types of productions such as photographic materials and radio and television programs.

18. Simple types of production such as the making of recordings will be done within individual schools.

Summary

The instructional materials center is a resource center for teaching tools, materials, and ideas. The service it renders is affected by the leadership ability and professional education of the person who directs it. The person in charge of an instructional materials center is called upon to render many services such as:

1. Stimulating and helping teachers, pupils, and others to make the most of instructional resources
2. Serving as a resource person for curriculum planning councils and other committees
3. Cataloging and organizing materials for use
4. Providing for cooperative exchange of services and materials
5. Assisting in formal and informal inservice education
6. Assisting in the use of instructional equipment
7. Providing mechanical and clerical services
8. Producing simple teaching materials.

These *services* must be *provided* by both school and school system centers, but the emphases vary in the two programs.

Certain basic instructional *services* must be *housed* in the individual school; however, many services may be housed in either individual schools or in school system centers. The decision naturally affects the housing needs of each. Materials and equipment used frequently and those which are inexpensive should always be housed in the individual school.

The necessary instructional materials services *may* be provided in schools where library materials and audio-visual materials are housed separately. They *may* also be provided in schools where the book and audio-visual materials are combined in one center. Regardless of the administrative pattern, adequate, properly arranged space, readily accessible thruout the day to pupils, teachers, and other members of the community, is essential.

HOUSING BASIC FUNCTIONS

Facilities must be provided for five basic functions in both single school buildings and in city or county centers.

1. Storage, handling, repair, and distribution of audio-visual materials
2. Storage, handling, care, and distribution of equipment
3. Production of materials
4. Preview and auditioning
5. Administration.

In general, the basic functions of the audio-visual instructional materials center in a single building are duplicated in a citywide or in a county center and similar building spaces should be provided for such centers. For the city or county center the repair, shipping, and storage spaces should be approximately double that provided for the individual building for each 15 buildings served regularly by the center. Likewise, centers which are regularly used by school-community groups or by non-school groups must be provided with additional and/or larger studios and production laboratories than the ones planned for the school instruction staff only.

It has been found advantageous in both the single school and the community center to provide for a "model" classroom. Such a space, which may very well be regularly used as a classroom, not only provides additional previewing, demonstrating, and meeting space at scheduled times but also serves as an experimental center for the evaluation and frequently the promotion of new materials, equipment, and procedures.

It is impossible to state specifically the facilities and amount of floor space which will adequately care for the instructional needs of a school or school system of a stated size. No two school systems have precisely the same needs. The diagrams presented here illustrate ways in which some communities have provided space for instructional materials centers.

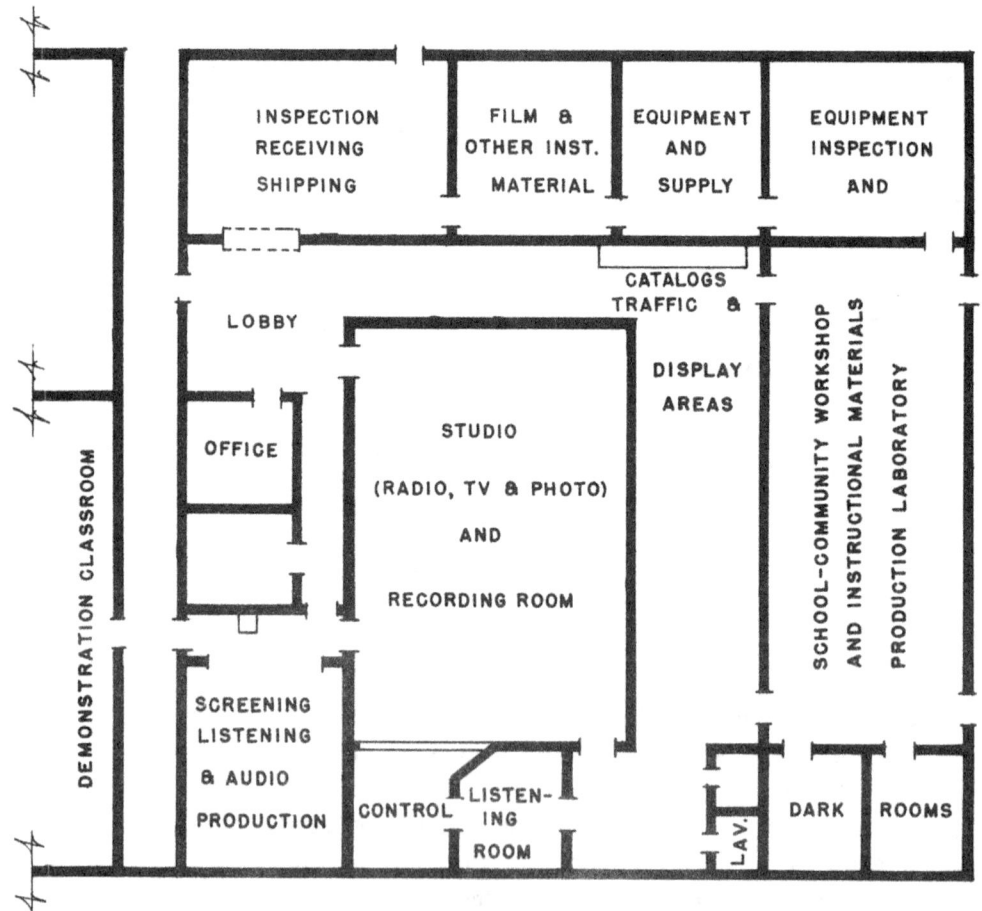

19. Diagram showing functional areas to be provided in an audio-visual instructional materials center for communities with 10-20 schools.

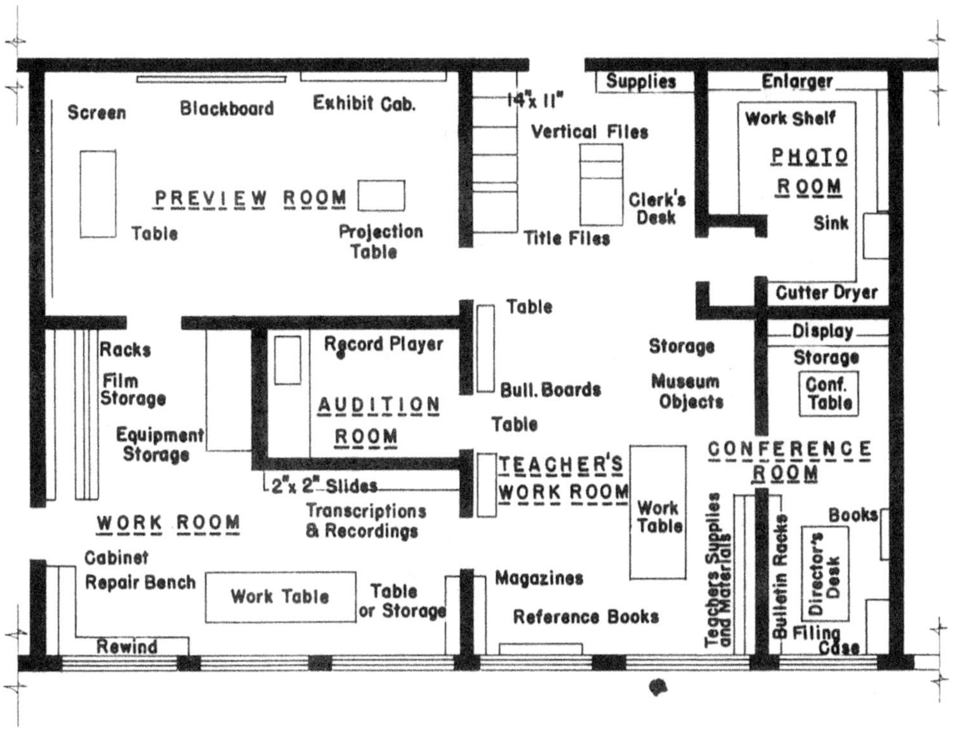

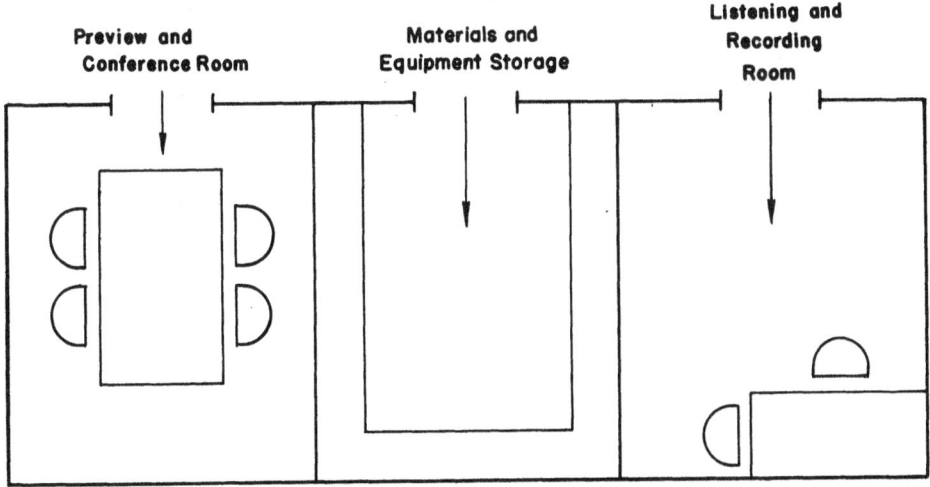

20. Suggested layout for a city audio-visual center.

21. The small elementary school may meet its needs with a few well equipped spaces. The indicated areas were planned to be adjacent to a teachers' workroom.

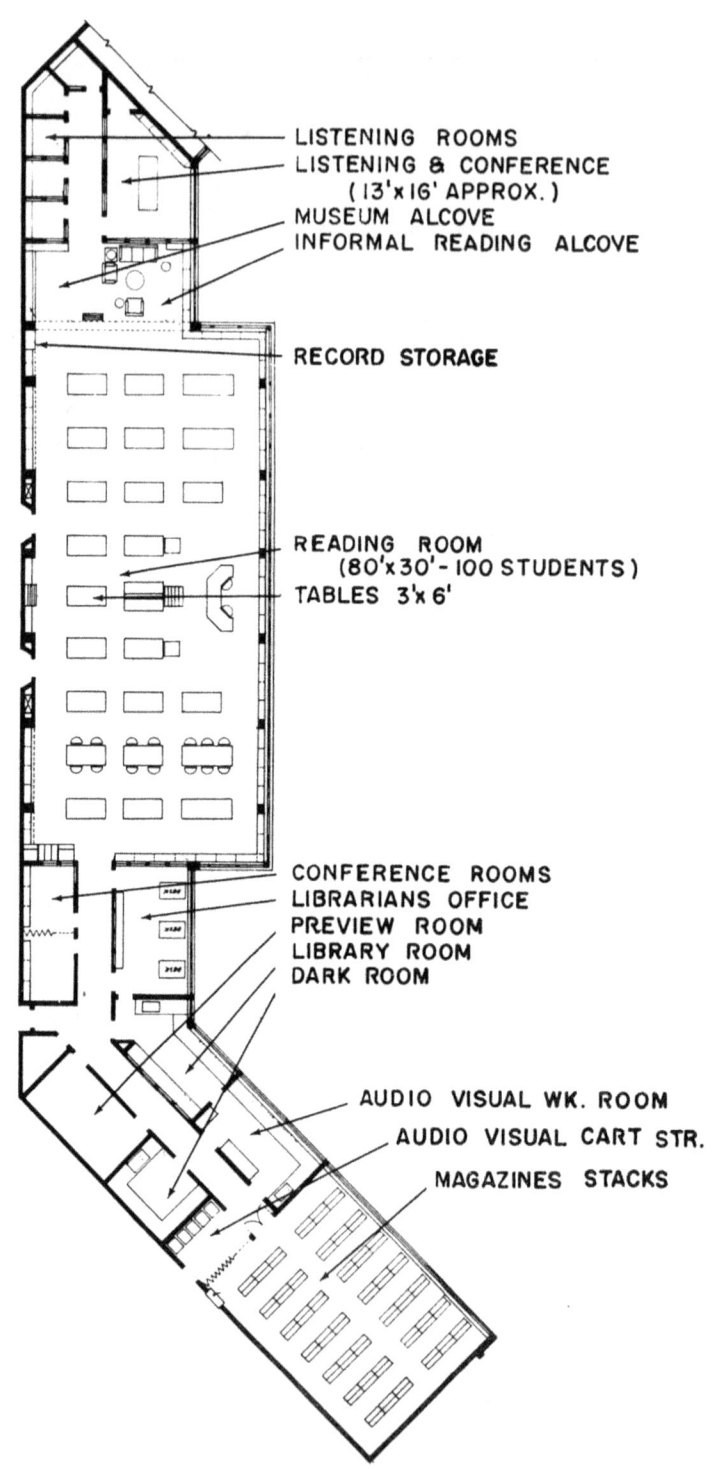

22. Layout for the instructional materials center of a high school in Chehalis, Washington, planned for 800 student capacity.

SUGGESTED
LIBRARY FOR A JUNIOR-SENIOR HIGH SCHOOL
ENROLLMENT 500

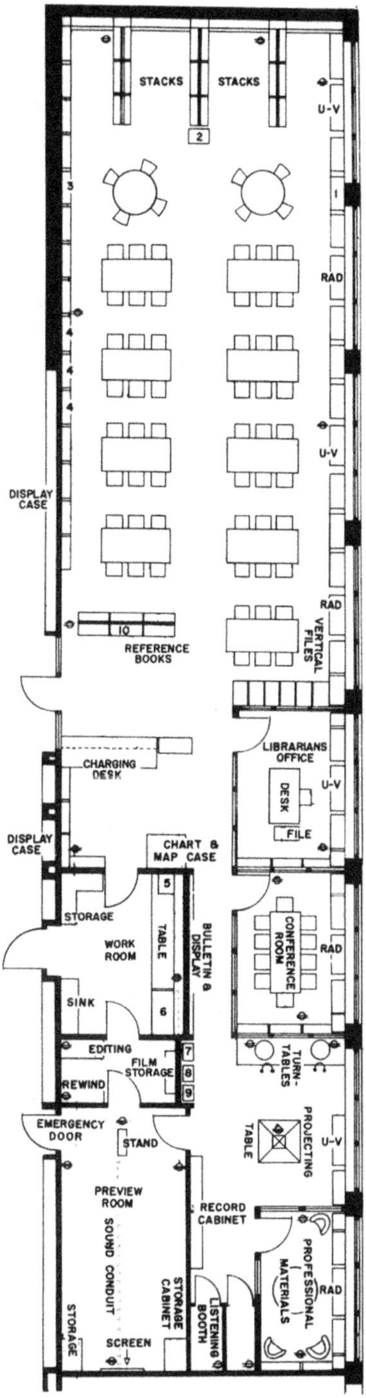

1. LOW SHELVING
2. DICTIONARY STAND
3. HIGH SHELVING
4. MAGAZINE & NEWSPAPER SHELVING
5. CARD CATALOG
6. DESK & TYPEWRITER TABLE
7. STRIP FILM
8. SLIDES
9. 16 INCH RECORD CABINET
10. COUNTER HEIGHT STACK

23. A library instructional materials center in a junior-senior high school with an enrollrollment of 500. Each classroom is equipped for audio-visual use. There is a photographic dark room in the science suite and a small radio studio in the speech department.

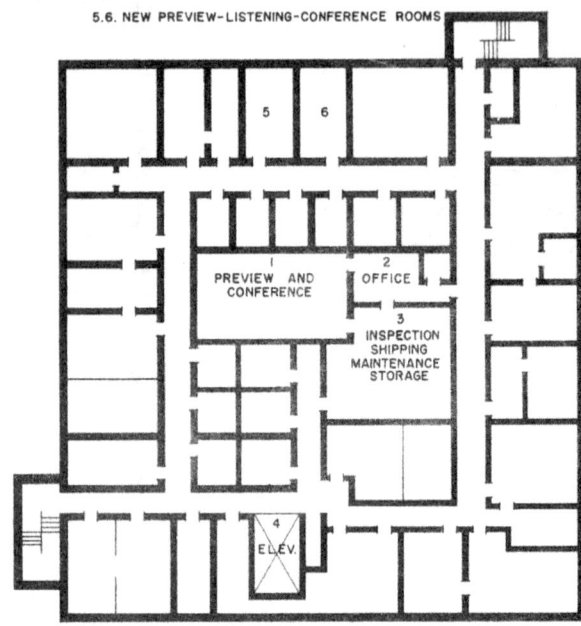

24. Teaching Materials Center, Arlington County Public Schools, Virginia.
   (a) Illustrates the location of the center in relation to other departments within the school system. On the same floor with the center are the offices of the supervisors, helping teachers, visiting teachers, psychological services, and the superintendent and his assistants.
   (b) Illustrates the location and layout for storage, handling, maintenance, repair, inspection, distribution, preview, and local production.

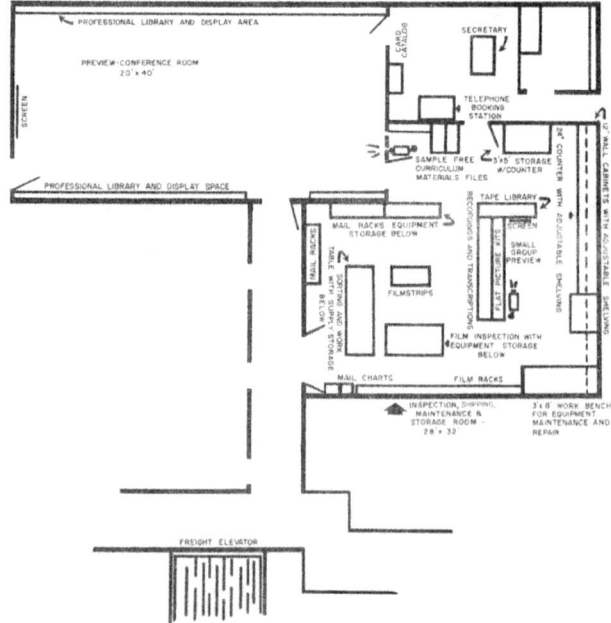

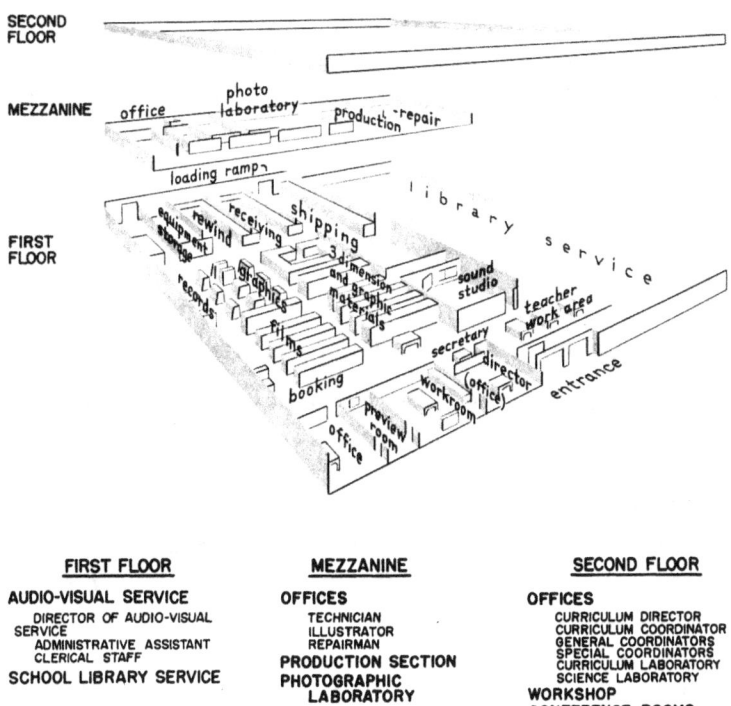

25. A schematic drawing of the space layout in the Audio-Visual Center of San Diego County, California.

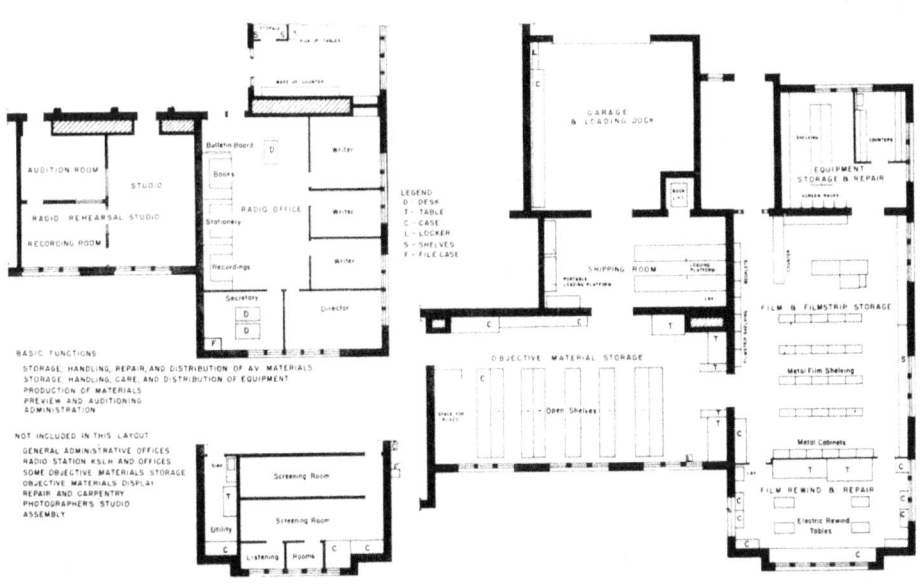

26. The housing of basic functions in the AV Instruction Materials Center of the St. Louis City Schools.

Space Needs

In the following pages generalized recommendations for space allocations are given, usually for a school of 600-1200 pupils. These figures represent averages based on the experience of audio-visual directors and can serve as guides to local planning groups.[3] Most building-planning committees tend to underestimate the space needs of instructional materials centers. *Remember that school buildings are used for many years.*

Storage, Handling, Repair, and Distribution of AV Materials

All materials and equipment supplied to the classroom teacher and pupils by the center should be stored in that center, or in spaces immediately adjacent to the center, except for those periods when they are in use in classrooms, or located in areas known to the staff and shown in the resources catalog of the center. The materials cannot be of service when they are unsystematically packed into overcrowded cupboards, stacked carelessly in cabinets, or piled in a corner. All materials should be stored so that they are easily accessible, both to those who wish to examine them and to those who wish to check them out for classroom use.

Included in this area and adapted to the particular needs of the school or community which the center serves should be such equipment and facilities as:

1. Large (legal size) file cabinet drawers for flat pictures
2. Shallow side drawer space for certain maps, charts, and larger pictures
3. Special cabinets or shallow drawer space for filmstrips
4. Special cabinets or shallow drawer space for slides and other transparencies
5. Special cabinets or cupboards for records
6. Special cabinets or cupboards for tape recordings
7. Special cabinets or cupboards for motion picture films
8. Special shelving for books and pamphlets.

---

[3]Schools or school systems planning instructional materials centers which will combine book and audio-visual materials should consult the publication *Dear Mr. Architect* for space needs and suggested layouts (4).

9. Sturdy tables with tools for opening and wrapping parcels. Such tables should provide recessed storage-cabinet space below.
10. Out-of-the-way but conveniently located storage for such things as shipping cases, reels, and cans
11. Sturdy table or tables (with nonmetallic tops) for inspecting, cleaning, repairing, and preparing for shipment or pickup, of all materials. Such tables should provide recessed storage-cabinet space below.
12. Adequate lighting without glare, including well shaded lights over worktable areas
13. Convenient electrical outlets
14. Good ventilation, including special fans and ducts for removing fumes during film-cleaning operations
15. Thermostatically controlled temperature with controlled humidity
16. Out-of-the-way but conveniently located storage for special tools, hardware, glues, and cleaner fluid needed in repair of materials
17. Nonsplash sink with quiet faucets
18. First-aid material for minor cuts
19. Package trucks and/or carts for moving heavy packages
20. Sturdy, lightweight stepladder
21. Compact "visual" cardfile
22. Minimum tack-board space on wall side of cabinets or shelving.

Such a list indicates the basic requirements of a small systemwide or of a large individual school building center. For any one system or school such a list should be viewed as a reference or checklist to be adapted to local needs and available building spaces.

Obviously, attempts to store in the center all the instructional materials with which a center deals would be not only unsuccessful but would be highly undesirable. Some of the chief functions of the center, those of expediting distribution, the promotion of wide use of many types of materials, the encouragement of individual initiative in seeking out and securing new materials and ways of using them, may be jeopardized if the center is primarily a depository and lending agency.

Recommended space allocation: An area of 300-400 square feet is usually adequate for a school of 600-1200 pupils.

Cataloging materials

27. Space and facilities must be provided for the cataloging of all kinds of materials.

Booking materials

28. Visual files of many kinds are available for bookings of materials. Making multiple carbons of the confirmation form saves retyping the information to obtain shipping and file copies.

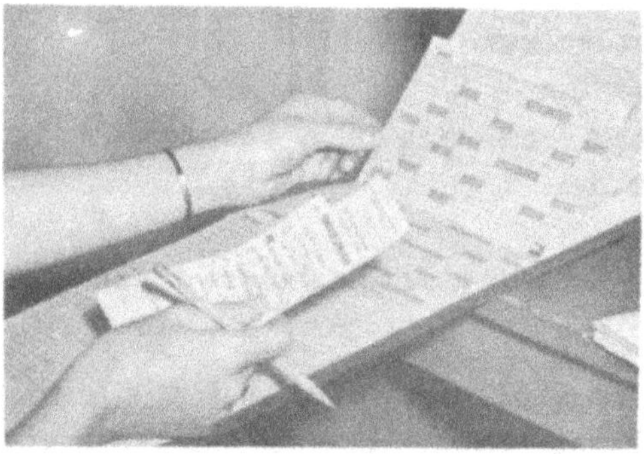

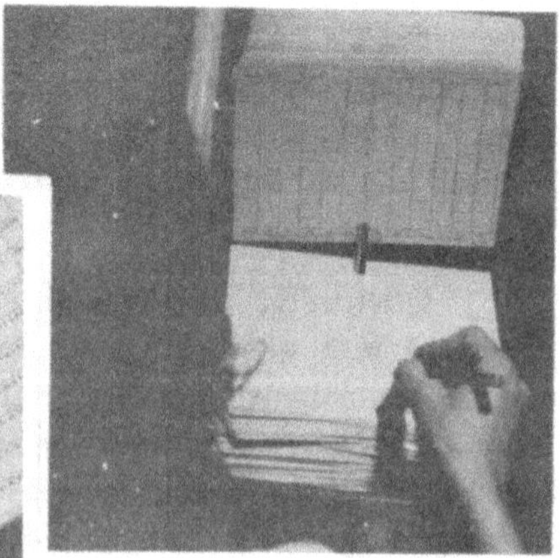

Shipping materials

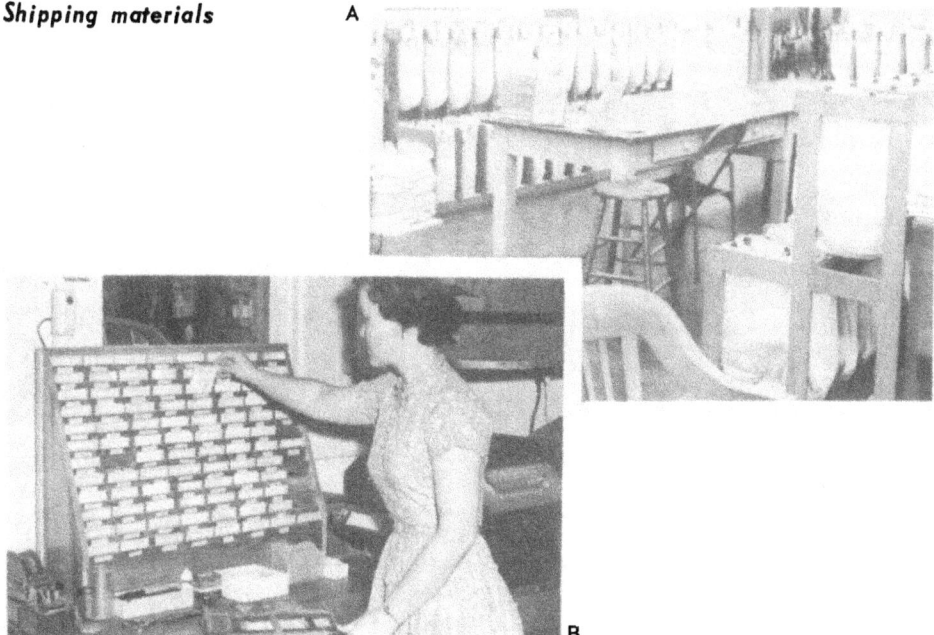

29. Sufficient space for the boxing and shipping of materials is especially important in the city or county center. (a) Some centers place packaged materials in mail bags to be delivered by truck. (b) Others find that the U. S. mail is the most economical method of distribution. Use of pre-addressed stickers saves time.

30. Storage facilities are needed in the shipping area for shipping cases, boxes, and other necessary equipment.

Repair of materials

31. A corner of the inspection and shipping area in a county center.

32. Provision for repair and materials storage in an individual school.

33. Film inspector using detector indicator to examine films for damage after their return from a user.

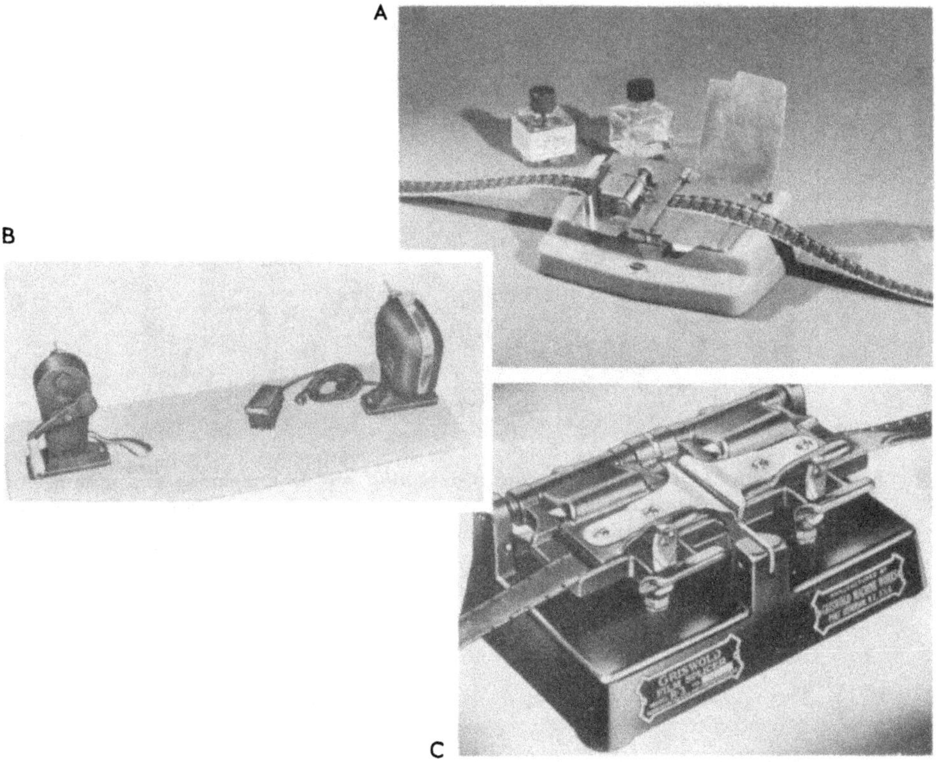

34. All school and school system centers will need splicers and rewinds. Some rewinds are run by electric motors.

35. Some centers use film cleaners which clean, polish, and rewind the film.

37

36. A complete film editing, faulty sprocket detecting, and film cleaning set-up is mounted on a plywood "lazy suzan." The segment is bolted at the rear, and pivots in a full half-circle so that any piece of equipment can be swung into position for use.

Storage of films

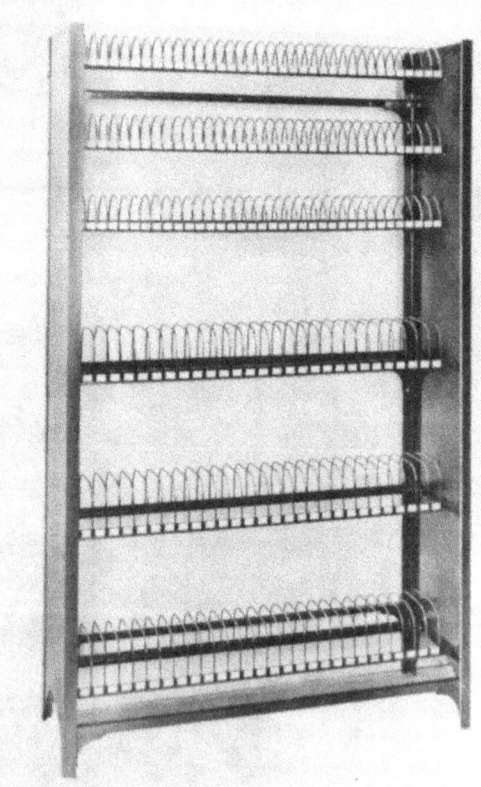

37. Film rack with capacity of 100-400 ft. 16 mm reels and 100-800, 1200, or 1600 ft. reels. Reinforced with cross braces front and back, drilled for mounting to wall or another unit. Overall size 48" wide, 72" high, 16" deep.

38. Metal film storage cabinets for 16 mm reels and cans. Overall size 29" wide, 66" high, 15" deep. Interior fitted with 5 film separator racks. Capacity of 20-400 ft. reels, 20-600 ft. reels, 20-800 ft. reels, 20-1200 ft. reels, 20-1600 ft. reels. Can be fitted with any combination of the above size reels.

39. Reel chests are convenient for storing and carrying small numbers of films.

Storage of filmstrips

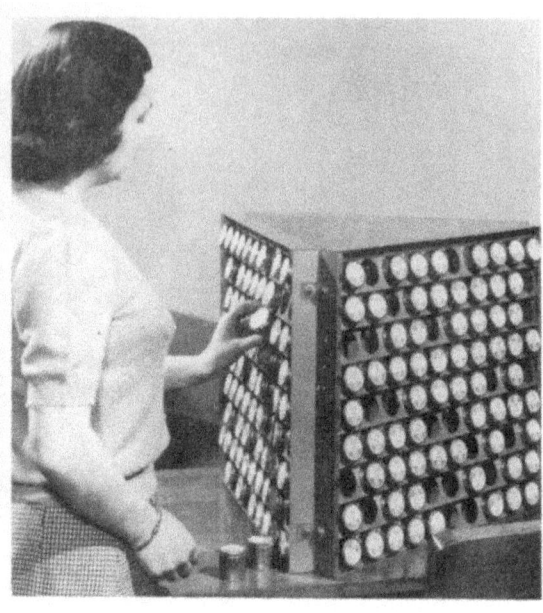

40. A filmstrip wall-file hangs securely on the wall, flat, using 2 key hole hangers. Capacity is 90 filmstrips. Overall size 7 3/4" high, 19 1/2" wide, 1 3/4" deep. Two or more wall-files can be placed together horizontally or vertically against a wall or bolted together to form table-files.

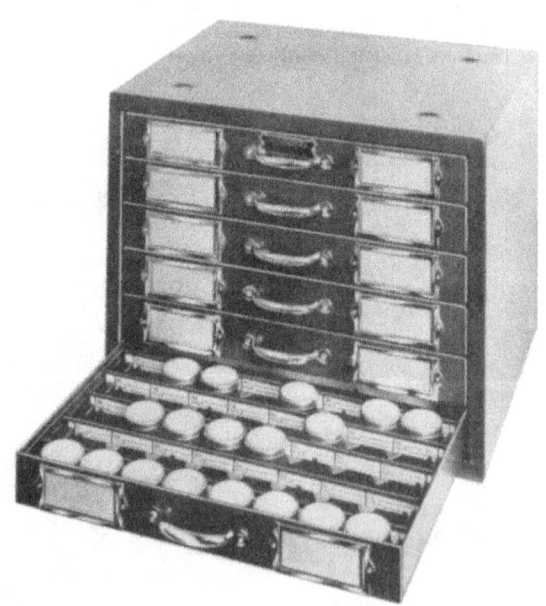

41. Steel cabinet to accommodate 336 filmstrips. Each of the 6 drawers have 7 adjustable dividers. Overall size 15" wide, 12" deep, 13" high.

42. Combination filmstrip and 16" transcription cabinet will hold approximately 75 filmstrips. Overall size 29" wide, 21 1/2" high, 17" deep.

43. Filmstrips are stored in the shipping cases used to send filmstrips from the center to the individual schools. Study guides are kept under the filmstrip boxes.

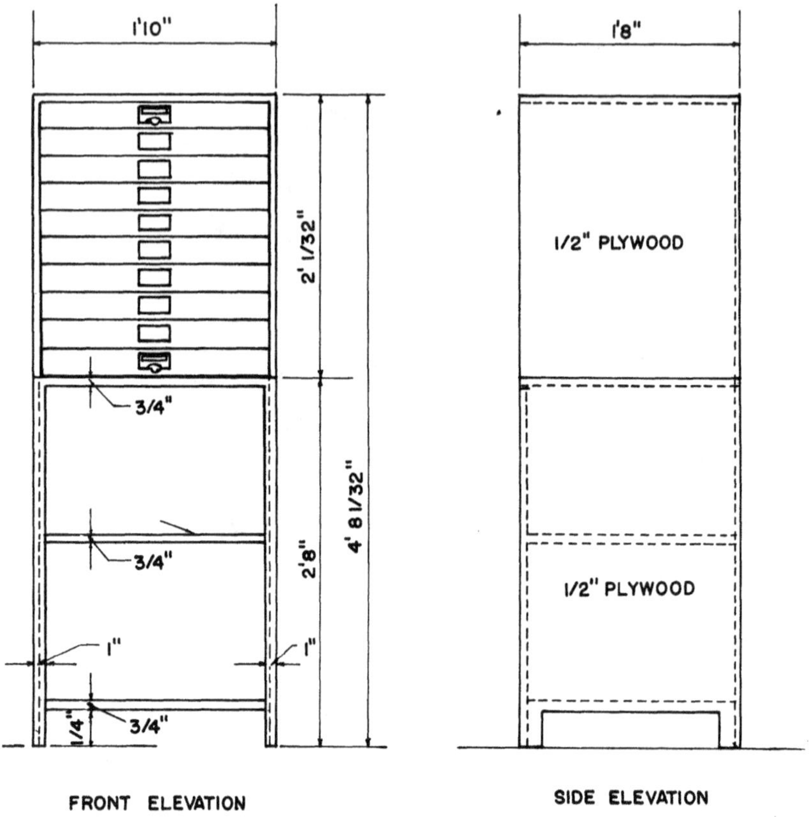

FRONT ELEVATION   SIDE ELEVATION

44. Details for the construction of a filmstrip storage cabinet.

Storage of records and tapes

45. A sectional tape recording cabinet. The cabinet for 5" reels is 13 1/8" wide, 12 5/8" high, and 8 5/8" deep with a capacity of 42 reels.

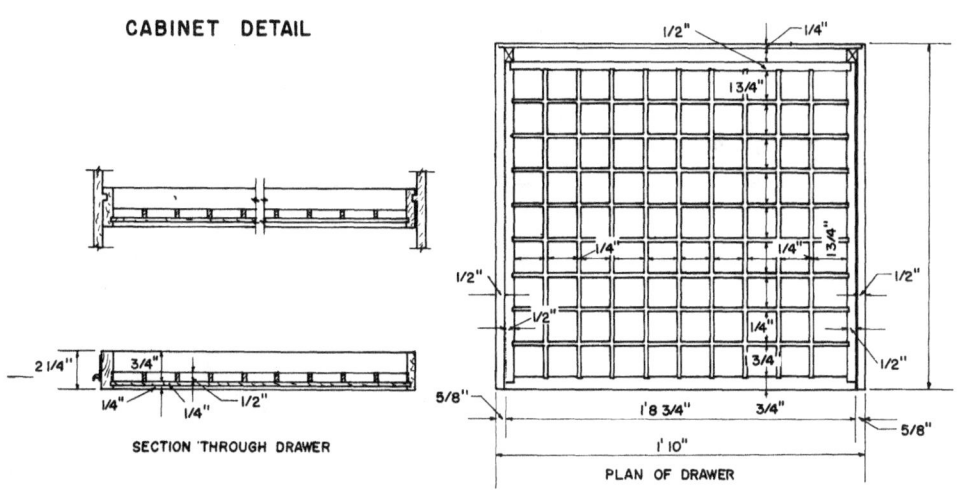

46. A double door tape recording cabinet. Overall size 29" wide, 52" high, and 10" deep. Will hold 384-5" reels or 288-7" reels.

47. Sectional disc cabinet available for 7", 10", 12", or 16" records. Total capacity 90 records.

48. Disc cabinet with double doors. Capacity 540 records. Overall size 29" wide, 52" high, 14" deep.

49. Cubicles for the storage of records and albums.

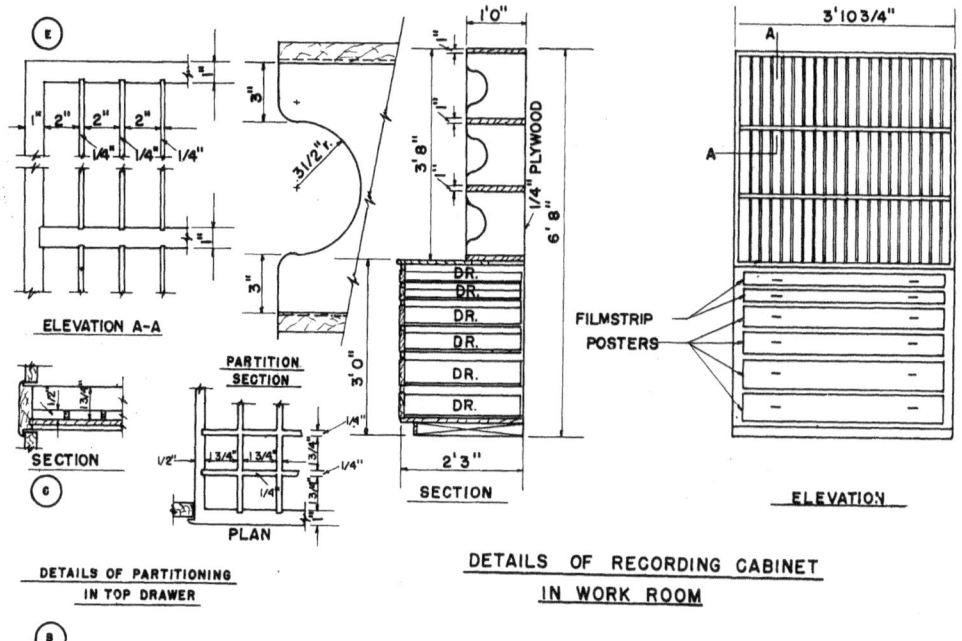

50. Details for the construction of a recording storage cabinet.

Storage of slides

51. Slide cabinets are available for the storage of 2x2 and 3¼x4 slides. The overall size of the cabinet shown is 15" wide, 12" deep, 13" high. Each slide in the drawer at the left is held in position for individual indexing. The drawer holds 250 glass slides or 500 readymounts. The drawer on the right has 30 adjustable index dividers. This drawer is designed for housing sets of slides. The drawer will hold 500 glass slides or 1000 readymounts.

52. These trays hold lantern slides vertically, so that titles on the top edge of the slides can be read. Capacity of this unit is approximately 1400 slides.

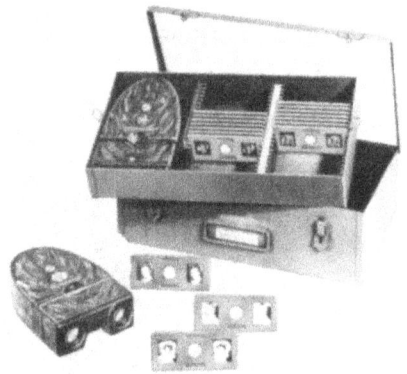

53. Many schools will want portable cases and storage cabinets for stereoscopes. The portable case shown will carry the viewer and 115 stereo slides.

54. Most schools will need several portable file boxes for slides and slide sets.

55. Slide sets may be stored in sturdy cardboard boxes and shipped in fiber cases.

Storage of charts, maps, and study prints

56. A suggested method for storing charts to facilitate their inspection and use.

57. A drawer file for storing charts, maps, and other flat materials. The drawers are 43" wide and 25 1/4" deep.

58. A homemade storage cabinet for filing of study print sets.

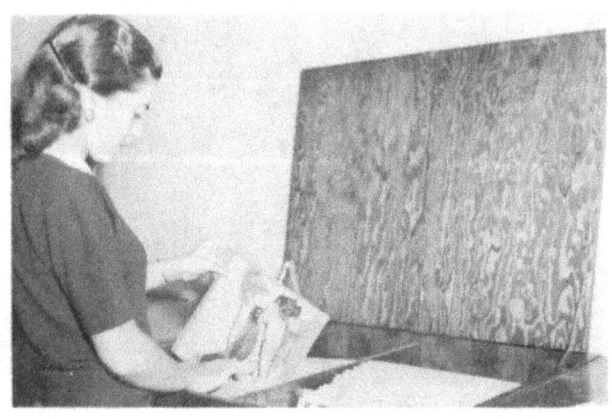

59. A homemade file for the storage of flat pictures.

Storage of exhibits and collections

60. Exhibit cases with glass doors and glass shelves are excellent for the display of objects and models.

61. A satisfactory homemade storage cabinet for scientific collections and exhibits.

Storage, Handling, Care, and Distribution of Equipment

As with materials, equipment should be easily accessible and should be kept in repair, ready for use. Adequate, dry, and well ventilated space, equipped with worktables and dustproof cupboards, should be provided for storage and servicing of equipment. This space must be well illuminated. Space should be provided in or adjacent to the center where teachers and students may come for instruction and practice in the operation of equipment. The equipment, storage, and servicing space should be arranged so as to provide easy access to a ground floor entrance available to delivery men and others.

For the building space used in storage, handling, care, and distribution of equipment, a list of special facilities should be prepared similar to the one suggested in the previous section on storage and distribution of materials. This list should include a number of storage racks and cabinets especially adapted to the several types of equipment used in the classroom, as well as storage cabinets for tools and supplies used in inspection, maintenance, and repair. In most cases, sufficient dry, dustproof space should be available to store all projection and recording equipment during the months in which the schools are closed. Such storage makes all equipment more accessible for inspection and repair in nonschool months.

Also in this area, one may expect to find sturdy, nonmetal tables for use in the inspection, testing, and repair of those pieces of equipment requiring electricity in their operation. Recessed storage cabinets may be built into the lower part of these tables. A number of electrical outlets and radio and television antenna outlets should be located conveniently near these tables.

Here, too, there should be readily available first-aid materials, hand-operated fire extinguishers, a sturdy stepladder, and proper tools and other equipment for routine servicing and shipping of equipment.

Recommended space allocation: An area of about 300 square feet is usually adequate for a school of 600-1200 pupils.

Equipment storage

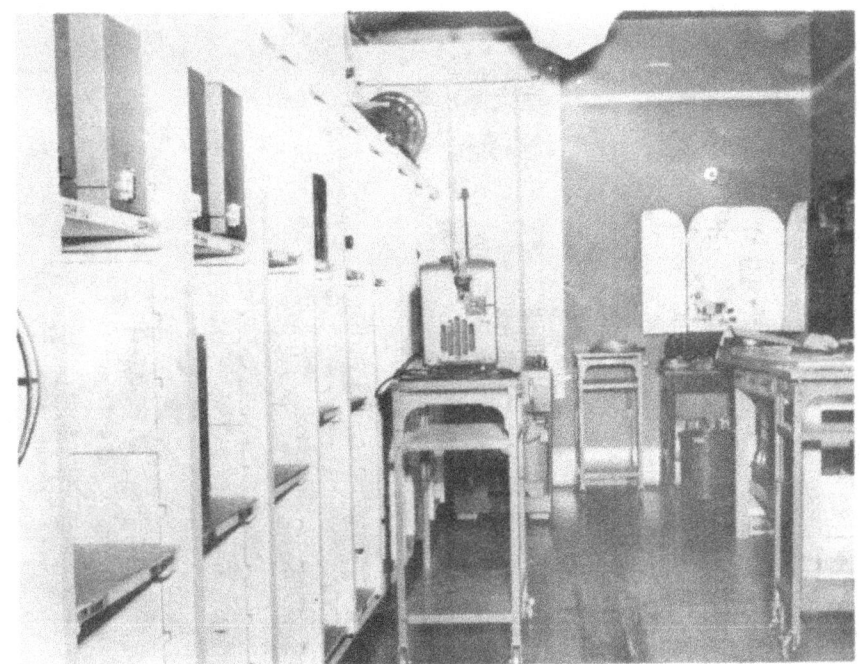

62. A well-organized equipment storage area.

63. Adequate equipment storage cabinets can be constructed by the Industrial Arts Department.

Equipment repair

64. An equipment maintenance area in a county audio-visual center.

65. Work space and equipment are essential for the checking and maintenance of equipment.

Transportation of equipment

A. B.

66. Movable projection stands with rubber wheels may be used in transporting equipment from the center to the classrooms.

67. A satisfactory homemade projection cart.

Production of Materials

Space should be provided at the center for the production of whatever materials are to be produced locally. Production space should be provided for photographic developing; for making recordings, slides, exhibits; for planning and producing radio and television programs; for art work; for mounting of pictures; and numerous other construction activities.

The production areas should be so planned and of such size as to allow for expansion of activity in the production of many types of materials and broadcasts. The school's rate of production in these areas before the establishment of proper facilities in a center is a far from accurate measure of the real needs or of the potential school-community activity in this important area.

Recommended space allocation: Two dark rooms, each 5'x10'. Radio and recording studio, 20'x20', with additional control-room space about 7'x10'. Large workshop, including graphics production area, 600-800 square feet. For television production, a studio of at least 30'x40' with a 15-foot ceiling adjacent to a prop storage room, approximately 20'x20'; a program planning space at least 10'x12'; and a control room with a minimum floor space of 7'x10'.

Production of radio programs

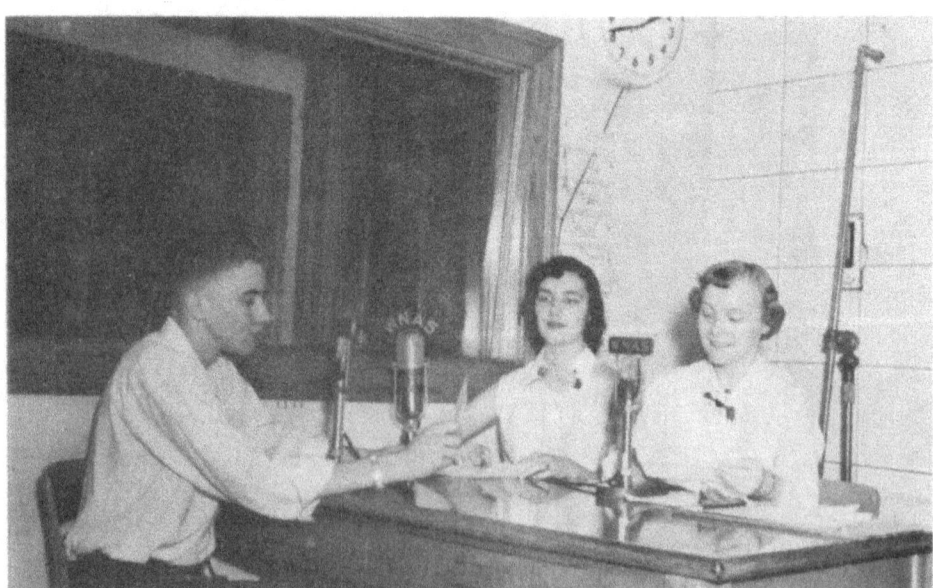

68. Students broadcasting from small radio studio in a city center.

69. Students using control room in a small radio production center.

Television production

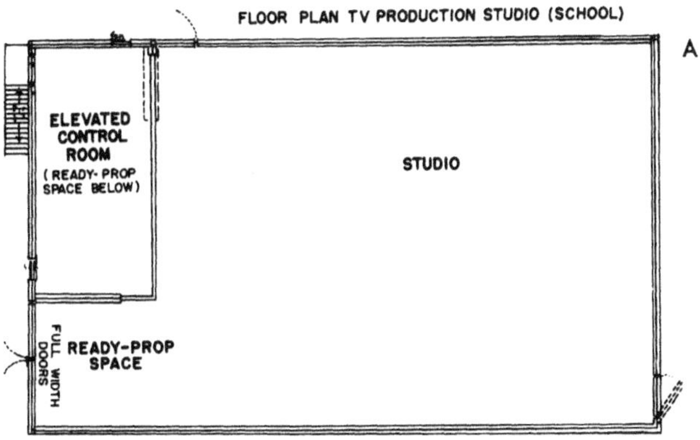

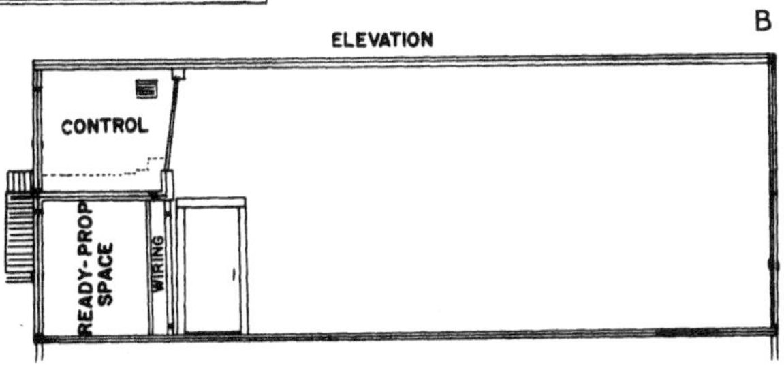

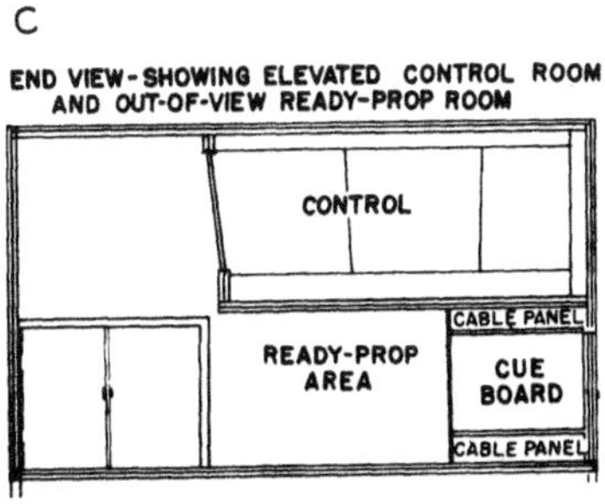

70. Suggest layout for a TV production studio.
    a. Floor plan.
    b. Elevation.
    c. End view, showing elevated control room and out-of-view ready-prop room.

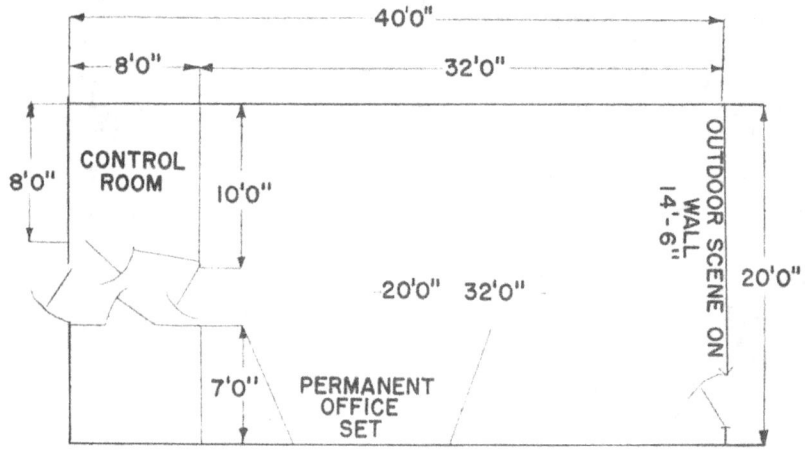

71. Suggested TV studio floor plan.

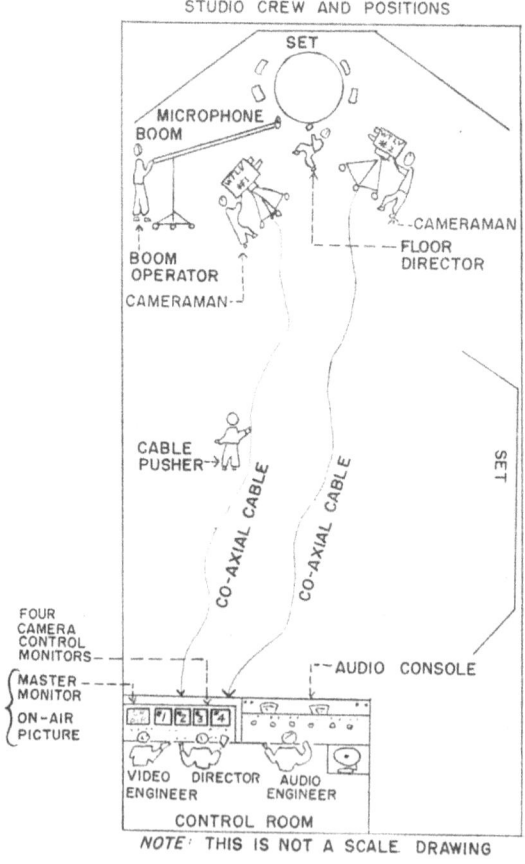

72. Schematic drawing showing minimum studio crew in position (not a scale drawing). A film camera in an additional area is not shown.

Photographic production

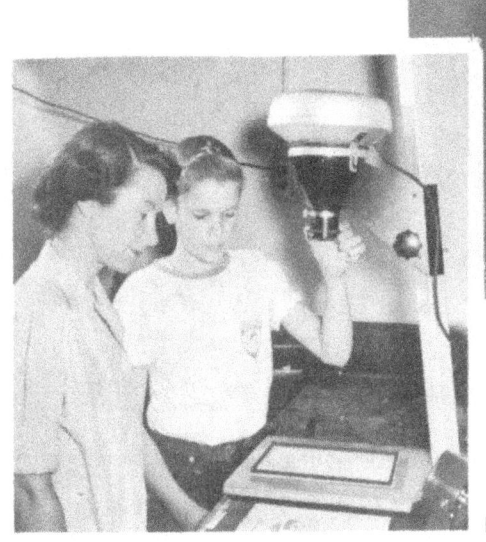

73. Dark rooms should be provided with the basic equipment for the developing, printing, and enlarging of photographs.

74. Centers in many school systems will want editing equipment and tables for use in the production of simple films.

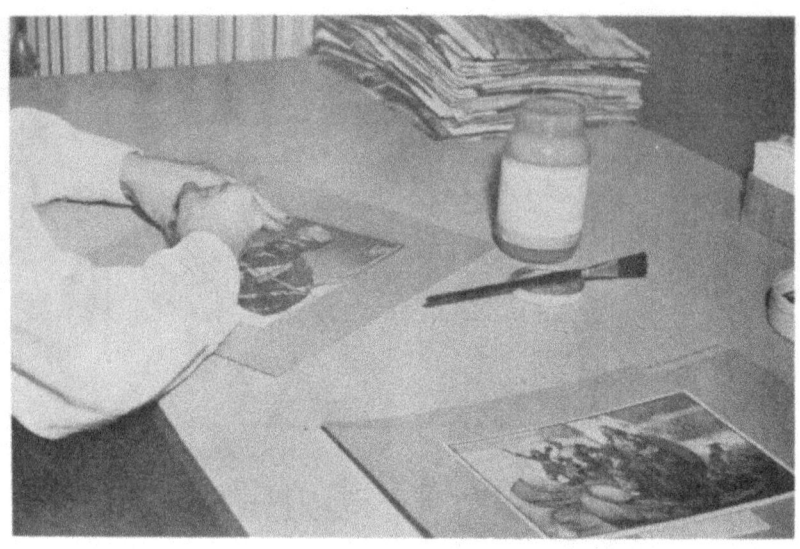

75. A large workroom is needed to accommodate the mounting of pictures, construction activities, and graphic arts production.

Preview and Auditioning

Convenient space and equipment provisions should be made for individuals and for small groups which serve as formal or informal committees for filmpreviewing, for auditioning records and recordings, for examining flat pictures and models, and for exploring and experimenting with many other materials of instruction.

This space, rather than be a small auditorium, should be a coordinated outlay of work areas for those concerned with the materials and activities of the whole instructional program. A group of small adjoining rooms is preferable to one large room. Such arrangements help avoid conflicts between individuals or groups of varying interests.

Small rooms for previewing films or listening to records, and larger laboratory areas equipped with highly adaptable tables, running water, and vertical display boards for making and experimenting with charts, maps, and many other types of material are essential. Suggestions for planning this space may be found in *Planning Schools for Use of Audio-Visual Materials: No. 1, Classrooms* (23). This space should also include room for the catalog files and for complete functional accommodation of those using the files.

Recommended space allocation: A total area of 800-1000 square feet is usually adequate for schools of 600-1200 pupils.

Previewing and auditioning

76. Movable, soundproof projector stand for use in a preview room.

77. Teacher auditions records for classroom use.

78. Listening tables are very useful. By using earphones, many persons can audition materials without disturbing one another.

Catalog files

A

B

79. Catalog files should be accessible to all persons wishing to select, preview or audition materials.

Administration

Office space should be provided for the coordinator and for the clerical and technical staff necessary to the carrying out of the program and to the maximum use of the center.

Such office space should be a separate but integral part of the building space allotted to the center. If the center's office is in another part of the building which houses the center, the person in charge is functionally handicapped. He should be readily accessible to users of the center and should not be remote from his office, his records, or his telephone when he is assisting others in the center.

Because many "outsiders" are normally using the facilities of a large school or systemwide center, an extra telephone instrument, in addition to the telephones in the center office but on one of the same lines, should be placed outside the office so that teachers and others in the center may use it without entering the office. For announcing incoming telephone calls and for other communication a simple intercom system should be installed between the director's office and several rooms or work areas of the center.

There should be no filing or storing of instructional materials and equipment in the director's office. Likewise, facilities outside the office should be available for demonstrations, for previewing, and for auditioning.

Immediately adjacent to the office, there should be a reception or waiting room.

Recommended space allocation: An area of about 150-200 square feet is usually adequate.

Summary

Altho the basic functions for which facilities must be provided are the same for all schools and school systems, no two schools or school systems have precisely the same space needs. Generally speaking the repair, shipping, and storage spaces for the city or county center should be approximately double that provided for the individual building for each 15 buildings served by the center.

The following generalized recommendations for space allocations will be useful as guides:

1. Storage, handling, repair, and distribution of audio-visual materials — 300-400 square feet for a school of 600-1200 pupils
2. Storage, handling, care, and distribution of equipment — 300 square feet for a school of 600-1200 pupils
3. Production of materials
    a. Two darkrooms, each 5'x10'
    b. Workshop including graphics production area, 600-800 square feet
    c. Radio and recording studio, 20'x20' with additional control-room space 7'x10'
    d. Television production studio of at least 30'x40' with a 15-foot ceiling adjacent to a prop storage room about 20'x20', a planning space at least 10'x12', and a control-room with a minimum size of 7'x10'
4. Preview and auditioning — 800-1000 square feet for a school of 600-1200 pupils
5. Administration — 150-200 square feet.

ACHIEVING GOALS

How does a school or a school system go about setting up a new audio-visual materials center or improving one already established?

Such a center should be conceived as an integral part of over-all curriculum planning. It must not be thought of as a "program" in itself. As a part of the curriculum program, the service center for the school or school system should reflect the philosophy and policies of that program. If curriculum planning is thought of as the responsibility of one or two specialists or administrators, the center will be a personally planned, "personality" centered service which must be initially and continuously "sold" to teachers and school patrons. On the other hand, if the center is an outgrowth of joint school-community study and work on curriculum improvement, it is more likely to be recognized as a joint undertaking with responsibility for its successful functioning shared by all who are affected by it — teachers, pupils, administrators, supervisors, parents, and laymen in the community. Such a situation is most favorable to the development of a good audio-visual instructional materials center.

What might be the steps in the development of an AV-IM center in a school system committed to a modern educational program in which everyone affected by curriculum plans has a voice in determining those plans?

Step One — A school-community curriculum council or a representative subcommittee of such a council should explore the learning experiences appropriate to the curriculum.

In this step agreement should be reached on at least a partial listing of these experiences in terms of the books, pictures, charts, films, field trips, sound recordings, and other activities and materials required to make them possible. At this stage it is important to clarify group thinking on what constitutes adequate instructional materials and to develop a realization of the possibilities for improving instruction offered by the virtually unlimited scope of materials and learning experiences.

Step Two — A school-community committee should further explore ways in which good use of available learning resources may be assured each class, including a detailed examination of ways in which an audio-visual materials center can assist this process.

It is desirable for committees or their representatives to visit other schools and school systems offering illustrations of services and facilities which have been effective in making possible good use of a wide variety of learning aids. At this time it is also desirable to bring in special consultants or resource people whose experience will help the committees evaluate the many possible ways of providing an adequate instructional materials program.

Later it is desirable for the committees to draw up a plan of the special school service structure which they believe will make possible the best teacher-student use of instructional materials of all kinds.

Opportunities should be provided for inservice education activities in which many classroom teachers will participate in order to broaden their acquaintance with and increase their skill in using many types of instructional materials. Such inservice education could parallel the exploration activities of school-community committees and could include workshop or laboratory experiences in the production and use of many kinds of materials. Some modern materials have been so inaccessible in some schools that effective use of them in these schools will probably require long and strenuous inservice learning and practice in their use on the part of many teachers. Thus, it is important that opportunities be provided which will enable teachers to see clearly the important contributions that modern tools for learning make possible.

Step Three — A specific, detailed proposal for the type of center, which the exploration and study activities of steps one and two have shown to be needed, should be developed.

At this point the teachers, pupils, supervisors, administrators, and their lay public should be well aware of their needs and should be ready to make and back up a concrete proposal for the type of instructional materials service *they want*. If their exploration has been complete and well directed, they should be in a position to:

1. Suggest the kinds of services they want the center to give and offer definite ideas concerning the structure of a service program.

2. Give specific criteria for the selection of needed personnel.
3. Submit a tentative budget for the establishment of the service.

Step Four — A continuing evaluating and steering committee for the instructional materials services of the school should be provided.

No plan for instructional materials services should be considered static or in any way permanent. A good AV-IM center is characterized by constant well calculated adaptation to new and newly discovered needs and to better ways of meeting these needs. Furthermore, it is equally important that the same cooperative interest of all teachers and pupils and of representative members of the lay public be obtained for these processes of evaluation and adaptation. To insure the continuing work of this committee, this same group, or a well selected subgroup of the larger committee, should continue to serve in an advisory capacity to the director or coordinator of the AV-IM center.

APPENDIX

BIBLIOGRAPHY

Books, Articles, Pamphlets

1. Acoustical Materials Association. *Theory and Use of Architectural Acoustical Materials.* New York: the Association, 1950. 20 p.
2. American Association of School Administrators. *American School Buildings.* Twenty-Seventh Yearbook. Washington, D. C.: the Association, a department of the National Education Association, 1949. 525 p.
3. American Association of School Administrators. *American School Curriculum.* Thirty-First Yearbook. Washington, D. C.: the Association, a department of the National Education Association. 1953. Chapter 11, "Materials and Construction in Relation to Utility," p. 183-216.
4. American Association of School Librarians. *Dear Mr. Architect.* Chicago: American Library Association, 1952. 15 p.
5. Association for Supervision and Curriculum Development. *Action for Curriculum Improvement.* Washington, D. C.: the Association, a department of the National Education Association, 1951. 244 p.

6. Audio-Visual Education Association of California. *Setting Up Your Audio-Visual Program.* Stanford: Stanford University Press, 1949. 34 p.

7. Bell and Howell Company. *Architects' Visual Equipment Handbook.* Chicago: the Company, 1945. 30 p.

8. Bolt, Richard H., and Newman, Robert B. "Architectural Acoustics: Basic Planning Aspects." *Architectural Record* 107: 165-168, 244, 246, 248; April 1950.

9. Brunstetter, Max R. "Housing an Audio-Visual Materials Center." *Nation's Schools* 34: 34-35; December 1944.

10. Bursch, Charles W., and Reid, John L. *You Want to Build a School?* New York: Reinhold Publishing Corp., 1947. p. 113-18.

11. Clapp, Wilfred F., and Perkins, Lawrence B. "Designing the School Plant for Multiple Use." *American School and University.* Eighteenth edition. New York: American School Publishing Corp., 1946. p. 69-74.

12. Cocking, Walter D., editor, *American School and University.* New York: American School Publishing Corp. Annual edition. (1951-52 issue has an extensive index of articles on school building facilities.)

13. Committee on Non-Theatrical Equipment. *Recommended Procedure and Equipment Specifications for Educational 16mm Projection.* New York: National Research Council, Committee on Scientific Aids to Learning, 54 p. (Reprinted from the *Journal of the Society of Motion Picture Engineers* for July 1941.)

14. Cravath, James R. "Lighting Projection Screen Surroundings." *Illuminating Engineering* 46: 361-64; July 1951.

15. Cravath, James R. "Projection Screen Surroundings." *Illuminating Engineering* 46: 9A, 12A; September 1951.

16. Cross, A. J. Foy. "Movies to Instructional Materials Centers." *Annual Bulletin No. 10.* Connecticut Audio-Visual Education Association, 1950. p. 39-44.

17. De Bernardis, Amo. "Adapting Old Buildings and Planning New Ones for the Effective Use of Audio-Visual Aids." *American School and University.* Fourteenth edition. New York: American School Publishing Corp., 1942. p. 259-64.

18. De Bernardis, Amo. "The Coordinator." *School Films.* p. 10, 11, 26-27; Spring 1948.

19. De Bernardis, Amo. "Tools For Teaching." *NEA Journal* 40: 552-54; November 1951.

20. Dent, Ellsworth C. "Plan Buildings for Visual Aids." *American School Board Journal* 107: 42-43; September 1943.

21. Dent, Ellsworth C. *The Audio-Visual Handbook.* Fourth edition. Chicago: Society for Visual Education, 1949, p. 185-95.

22. Department of Audio-Visual Instruction. *DAVI Boston Conference Proceedings 1952.* Washington, D. C.: the Department, National Education Association, 1952. p. 15-16. (Mimeo.)

23. Department of Audio-Visual Instruction. *Planning Schools for Use of Audio-Visual Materials: No. 1, Classrooms.* Second revised edition. Washington, D. C.: the Department, National Education Association, 1953. 40 p.

24. Department of Audio-Visual Instruction. *Planning Schools for Use of Audio-Visual Materials: No. 2, Auditoriums.* Washington, D. C.: the Department, National Education Association, 1953. 36 p.

25. Elliott, Godfrey, editor. *Film and Education.* New York: Philosophical Library, 1948. 597 p.

26. Englehardt, N. L.; Englehardt, N. L., Jr.; and Leggett, Stanton. *Planning Secondary School Buildings.* New York: Reinhold Publishing Corp., 1949. 252 p.

27. Harcleroad, Fred F., and Allen, William H., editors. *Audio-Visual Administration.* Dubuque, Iowa: William C. Brown Co., 1951. 118 p.

28. Hearn, Edward; Jones, John; and Morrison, Jack. "Name Your Poison." *American School and University.* Twenty-first edition. New York: America School Publishing Corp., 1949. p. 200-207.

29. Illuminating Engineering Society, and American Institute of Architects. *American Standard Practice for School Lighting.* New York: Illuminating Engineering Society, 1948. 79 p.

30. Kinder, James S. *Audio-Visual Materials and Techniques.* New York: American Book Co., 1950. p. 549-51.

31. Kolb, Frederick J., Jr. "Screen Brightness." *Journal of the Society of Motion Picture and Television Engineers* 56: 433-42; April 1951.

32. Kolb, Frederick J., Jr. "Specifying and Measuring the Brightness of Motion Picture Screens." *Journal of the Society of Motion Picture and Television Engineers* 61:533-42; October 1953.

33. Long, Paul E. "Designing the School Building for Effective Use of Audio-Visual Aids." *American School and University.* Seventeenth edition. New York: American School Publishing Corp., 1945. p. 117-18.

34. McPherson, James. "Patterns for Tomorrow." *See and Hear* 1: 78; February 1946.

35. Millgate, Irvine H., and Coelln, O. H., Jr. "Standards for Visual and Auditory Facilities in New Educational Buildings." *American School and University.* Eighteenth edition. New York: American School Publishing Corp., 1946. p. 136-51.

36. National Association of Radio and Television Broadcasters. *The Planning and Construction of Television Broadcasting Stations.* Washington, D. C.: the Association, 1952. 33 p.

37. National Council on School House Construction, Plant Guide Committee. *Guide for Planning School Plants, 1949.* Nashville: the Council (Sec.: W. D. McClurkin, George Peabody College for Teachers), 1949. 173 p.

38. National Education Association, Research Division. "Audio-Visual Educa-

tion in City-School Systems." *Research Bulletin* 24: 131-70; December 1946.

39. National Fire Protection Association. *Building Exit Codes.* Eleventh edition. Boston: the Association, 1951. 136 p.

40. New Jersey State Department of Education. *Thinking Television.* New Brunswick: the Department, 1953. 17 p. (Mimeo.)

41. Noel, Francis W. *Projecting Motion Pictures in the Classroom.* Motion Pictures in Education, Vol. 4, No. 5. Washington, D. C.: American Council on Education, 1940. 53 p.

42. Olney, Benjamin. "Acoustics of School Building." School Plant Studies Series. *Bulletin of The American Institute of Architects* 6: 17-20; November-December 1952.

43. Oregon Audio-Visual Association. *Recommended Minimum Standards for Instructional Materials Programs in Oregon Public Schools.* Salem: Oregon State Department of Public Instruction, 1952. 8 p. (Mimeo.)

44. Oregon State Department of Public Instruction. *Audio-Visual Aids in Oregon,* Salem: the Department, 1952. 30 p.

45. Perkins, Lawrence B., and Cocking, Walter D. *Schools.* New York: Reinhold Publishing Corp., 1949. 264 p.

46. Pryor, Richard W., editor. *The Audio-Visual Equipment Directory.* Evanston, Ill.: National Audio-Visual Association, 1953. 140 p.

47. Radio Corporation of America. *The Architects Manual of Engineered Sound Systems.* Camden: the Corporation, 1947. 288 p.

48. Radio Corporation of America. *Broadcast Equipment.* Camden: the Corporation, 1952. 12 p.

49. Reavis, William C. "Functional Planning of School-Buidling Programs." *Elementary School Journal* 46: 72-80; October 1945.

50. Rufsvold, Margaret I. *Audio-Visual School Library Service.* Chicago: American Library Association, 1949. p. 69-78.

51. Schreiber, Robert E., and Calvert, Leonard. *Building an Audio-Visual Program.* Chicago: Science Research Associates, 1946. 103 p.

52. Schwarz, Karl R. "Technical Considerations in Relation to Housing the Audio-Visual Program." *Bulletin of the School of Education, Indiana University* 22: 16-20; July 1946.

53. See and Hear. "Designs for Visual Education." *See and Hear* 4: 17-24; November 1948.

54. Smith, Henry Lester. "Trends That Affect Building." *Nation's Schools* 37: 35-37; May 1946.

55. Society of Motion Picture and Television Engineers. "Screen Brightness

Symposium." *Journal of the Society of Motion Picture and Television Engineers* 61: 213-72; August 1953, Part II.

56. Terlouw, Adrian L. "Planning for Audio-Visual Education." *Architectural Record* 98: 72-78; September 1945.

57. University of the State of New York, Division of School Buildings and Grounds. *Housing the Audio-Visual Program.* Albany: the University, 1946. 14 p.

58. U. S. Office of Education, and Radio-Television Manufacturers Association on the Use of Communications Equipment in Education. *Teaching with Radio, Audio, Recording, and Television Equipment.* Washington, D. C.: U. S. Office of Education, 1953. 41 p.

59. Waddill, George M. "Don't Blame the Architect." *School Executive* 61: 32-33; November 1941

60. Washington State Department of Public Instruction. *A Temporary Guide for the Instructional Materials Program.* Olympia: the Department, 1950. 52 p.

61. Will, Philip, Jr. "Audio-Visual Classroom Planning." *Architectural Record* 99: 66-77; February 1946.

62. Wittich, Walter A., and Schuller, Charles F. *Audio-Visual Materials,* New York: Harper and Brothers, 1953. 564 p.

Motion Pictures

63. *Audio-Visual Aids to Learning.* 16mm, sound, black and white, 11 min. Government Films Department, United World Films, Inc., 1445 Park Avenue, New York 29, N. Y., 1950.

64. *Better Schools for Rural Wisconsin.* 16mm, sound, color, 29 min. University of Wisconsin, Photographic Laboratory, 1208 West Johnson Street, Madison 6, Wis., 1948.

65. *Building For Learning.* 16mm, sound, color, 19 min. Agricultural and Mechanical College of Texas, Department of Architecture, College Station, Texas, 1951.

66. *Design for Learning.* 16mm, sound, color, 20 min. Photo and Sound, 116 Natoma Street, San Francisco 5, Calif., 1941.

67. *The Teaching Materials Center.* 16mm, sound, color or black and white, 9 min. Virginia State Department of Education, Richmond 16, Va., 1950.

68. *Using Visual Aids in Training.* 16mm, sound, black and white, 14 min. Government Films Department, United World Films, Inc., 1445 Park Avenue, New York 29, N. Y., 1944.

Filmstrips

69. *Audio-Visual Education Series.* Color. *The AV Building Representative,* 43 frames. (Other titles will be available in 1954.) McGraw-Hill Book Co., Text-Film Department, 330 West 42nd Street, New York 18, N.Y., 1953-54.

70. *Cooperative School Plant Planning.* Color, 100 frames, Indiana University, Audio-Visual Center, Bloomington, Ind., 1952.

71. *School Building.* Black and white, 145 frames, American Association of School Administrators, National Education Association, 1201 16th Street, N. W., Washington, D. C., 1953.

72. *School Buildings and Equipment.* Black and white, Part I — Elementary Schools, 55 frames; Part II — Secondary Schools, 58 frames; American Council on Education, 1785 Massachusetts Avenue, N. W., Washington, D. C., 1952.

73. *School Library Quarters.* Color, 98 frames, American Library Association, 50 East Huron Street, Chicago, Ill., 1952.

74. *What's So Important About Audio-Visual Aids.* Color, 52 frames, National Audio-Visual Association, Inc., 2540 Eastwood Avenue, Evanston, Ill., 1951.

75. *Audio-Visual Aids Series.* Black and white. *The Large City A-V Aids Organization,* 44 frames; *The Small City A-V Aids Department,* 40 frames; *The College Audio-Visual Center,* 37 frames; *The County Audio-Visual Service Program,* 54 frames; Young America Films, Inc., 18 E. 41st Street, New York 17, N. Y., 1949.

Slide Sets, 2" x 2"

76. *Planning Schools for Use of Audio-Visual Materials.* Black and white, Department of Audio-Visual Instruction, National Education Association, 1201 16th Street, N. W., Washington, D. C.

77. Sets produced by school systems illustrating audio-visual programs in action may be borrowed from the Department of Audio-Visual Instruction, National Education Association, 1201 16th Street, N. W., Washington, D. C.

   a. Grosse Pointe, Michigan
   b. Fulton County, Georgia
   c. Parma, Ohio

BRIEF LIST OF COMPANIES MANUFACTURING AND/OR DISTRIBUTING AUDIO-VISUAL EQUIPMENT FOR USE IN MATERIALS CENTERS

(The figures following the company names indicate the types of products manufactured or distributed: (1) Metal cabinets, rewinds, films, filmstrips, cleaners, and accessories; (2) Disc cabinets, tape machines, and accessories; (3) Transcription and record players, recorders, playbacks, records, tapes, and sound systems; (4) Projectors and accessories; (5) Tables, cabinets, desks, stands, mailing cases; (6) Projection screens; (7) Slide materials, bindings, accessories; (8) Walls, display boards, cupboards, floortiling, linoleum; (9) Air conditioning and temperature control.)

American Optical Company Instrument Division Box A Buffalo 15, New York	4
Ampro Corporation 2835 North Western Avenue Chicago 18, Illinois	4
Amstrong Cork Company Lancaster, Pennsylvania	8
Audio Devices, Inc. 444 Madison Avenue New York 22, New York	3
Audio-Master Corporation 17 East 45th Street New York 17, New York	3
Audio-Visual Supply Company 247 Broadway Laguna Beach, California	1
Austral Sales Corporation 101 Park Avenue New York 17, New York	5, 8
Automatic Projection Corporation 29 West 35th Street New York 1, New York	4
Bangor Cork Company William and D Streets Pen Argyl, Pennsylvania	8
Barnett and Jaffe 6100-10 North 21st Street Philadelphia 38, Pennsylvania	1, 5
Bausch and Lomb Optical Company 635 St. Paul Street Rochester 2, New York	4
Bavinco Manufacturing Company 400 Scajaquada Street Buffalo 11, New York	5, 8
Bell and Howell Company 7118 McCormick Road Chicago 45, Illinois	4
Charles Beseler Company 60 Badger Avenue Newark 8, New Jersey	4

Blank and Company 230 Park Avenue New York 17, New York	8
Brumberger 34 Thirty-fourth Street Brooklyn 32, New York	4, 7
Burke and James, Inc. 321 South Wabash Avenue Chicago 4, Illinois	3, 4
Califone Corporation 1041 North Sycamore Los Angeles 38, California	3
Celotex Corporation 120 South La Salle Street Chicago, Illinois	8
W. D. Clapp Company 333 North Michigan Avenue Chicago 1, Illinois	5
Claridge Equipment Company 4608 West 20th Street Chicago 50, Illinois	8
Jack C. Coffey Company 1124 Greenleaf Wilmette, Illinois	1, 5
Commercial Picture Equipment, Inc. 1567 West Homer Street Chicago 22, Illinois	1, 5
Compco Corporation 2251 West St. Paul Avenue Chicago 47, Illinois	1, 5
Craig Movie Supply Corporation 149 New Montgomery Street San Francisco 5, California	1
Crestwood Recorder Corporation 221 North La Salle Street Chicago 1, Illinois	3
Da-Lite Screen Company, Inc. 2711 North Pulaski Road Chicago 39, Illinois	6
De Vry Corporation 1111 Armitage Avenue Chicago 14, Illinois	4

Du Kane Corporation 4
St. Charles, Illinois

Eastman Kodak Company 4, 5
343 State Street
Rochester 4, Illinois

Electro-Chemical Products Corporation 1
60 Franklin Street
East Orange, New Jersey

Electro Engineering & Manufacturing
   Company 4
Illustravox Division
627 West Alexandrine
Detroit 1, Michigan

Extendoor, Inc. 8
Muskegon, Michigan

Eye Gate House, Inc. 3, 4
2716 Forty-first Avenue
Long Island City 1, New York

Fiberbilt Case Company 5
40 West 17th Street
New York 11, New York

Forway Industries, Inc. 4
245 West 55th Street
New York 19, New York

The F R Corporation 4
951 Brook Avenue
New York 56, New York

GoldE Manufacturing Company 4
4888 North Clark Street
Chicago 40, Illinois

Gotham Chalkboard & Trim Company,
   Inc. 8
246 East 125th Street
New York 35, New York

Hamilton Electronics Corporation 3
2726 Pratt Avenue
Chicago 45, Illinois

The Harwald Company 1, 4
1216 Chicago Avenue
Evanston, Illinois

International Business Machines

Corporation 5
590 Madison Avenue
New York 22, New York

Johns-Manville 8
22 East 40th Street
New York 16, New York

Johnson Temperature Control Company 9
Milwaukee 2, Wisconsin

Keystone View Company 4
Meadville, Pennsylvania

Masco Electronic Sales Corporation 3
32-28 Forty-ninth Street
Long Island City 3, New York

O. J. McClure Talking Pictures 3, 4
1115 West Washington Boulevard
Chicago 7, Illinois

Minneapolis-Honeywell Regulator
    Company 9
2753 Fourth Avenue, South
Minneapolis, Minnesota

Minnesota Mining & Manufacturing
    Company 3
St. Paul 6, Minnesota

Monson Corporation 3
919 North Michigan Avenue
Chicago, Illinois

Movie-Mite Corporation 4
1116 Truman Road
Kansas City 6, Missouri

Moviola Manufacturing Company 1
1451 Gordon Street
Hollywood 28, California

Mutschler Brothers Company 8
Nappanee, Indiana

Natural Slate Blackboard Company 8
Pen Argyl, Pennsylvania

Neumade Products Corporation 1, 5
330 West 42nd Street
New York 36, New York

Newcomb Audio Products Company 3

6824 Lexington Avenue
Hollywood 38, California

New Castle Products   8
New Castle, Indiana

New York Silicate Book Slate Company   8
541 Lexington Avenue
New York 22, New York

New York Standard Blackboard
    Company, Inc.   8
225 Broadway
New York 7, New York

Penn Big Bed Slate Company   8
Slatington, Pennsylvania

Pennsylvania Slate Producers Guild,
    Inc.   8
205 Realty Building
Pen Argyl, Pennsylvania

Pentron Corporation   3
221 East Cullerton Street
Chicago 16, Illinois

Projectograph Corporation   4
23 Church Street
Oshkosh, Wisconsin

Prothmann, Konrad   5
7 Soper Avenue
Baldwin, Long Island, New York

Radiant Manufacturing Company   6
2627 West Roosevelt Road
Chicago 8, Illinois

Radio Corporation of America   4
RCA-Victor Division
Camden, New Jersey

Reeves Soundcraft Corporation   3
10 East 52nd Street
New York 22, New York

Rek-O-Kut Company   3
38-01 Queens Boulevard
Long Island City 1, New York

Remington Rand, Inc.   5
315 Fourth Avenue
New York 10, New York

Revere Camera Company 320 East 21st Street Chicago 16, Illinois	3, 4
Rowles Company Arlington Heights, Illinois	8
Society for Visual Education, Inc. 1345 West Diversey Parkway Chicago 14, Illinois	4, 7
Spindler and Sauppe 2201 Beverly Boulevard Los Angeles 4, California	4
Squibb-Taylor, Inc. 1213 South Akard Street Dallas 1, Texas	4
Standard Projector & Equipment Company, Inc. 7106 Tuohy Avenue Chicago 31, Illinois	4
David Stoddard & Sons Bangor, Pennsylvania	8
Strong Electric Corporation 87 City Park Avenue Toledo 2, Ohio	4
Television Associates East Michigan Street Michigan City, Indiana	4
Three Dimension Company 4555 West Addison Street Chicago 41, Illinois	4
United States Plywood Corporation 55 West 44th Street New York 17, New York	8
Victor Animatograph Corporation Davenport Bank Building Davenport, Iowa	4
Victorlite Industries, Inc. 5350 Second Avenue Los Angeles 43, California	4
Viewlex, Inc. 35-01 Queens Boulevard Long Island City 1, New York	4

Vita-Lite Screen Company 239 A Street San Diego 1, California	6
Wallach and Associates 1532 Hillcrest Road Cleveland 18, Ohio	2
Webster Electric Company 1900 Clark Street Racine, Wisconsin	3
Webster-Chicago Corporation 5610 West Bloomingdale Chicago 39, Illinois	3
The Wiethoff Company 1712 First Street San Fernando, California	5
Young America Films, Inc. 18 East 41st Street New York 17, New York	4

For additional information consult:

Planning Schools for Use of Audio-Visual Materials — No. 1, Classrooms. Department of Audio-Visual Instruction, National Education Association, 1201 16th Street, N. W., Washington, D. C. (Appendix contains a list of companies producing and/or distributing light control materials and equipment.)

Planning Schools for Use of Audio-Visual Materials — No. 2, Auditoriums. Department of Audio-Visual Instruction, National Education Association, 1201 16th Street, N. W., Washington, D. C. (Appendix contains a list of companies manufacturing audio-visual equipment for auditorium use.)

Joint Committee on Educational Television, 1785 Massachusetts Avenue, N. W., Washington 6, D. C.

Radio-Television Service, U. S. Office of Education, Department of Health, Education, and Welfare, Washington 25, D. C.

PRICE LIST

Single copy	$1.00
2 to 9 copies	10% discount
10 to 99 copies	25% discount
100 and over	33 1/3% discount

What Is Your School's I.M. Quotient?

DOES YOUR SCHOOL HAVE ADEQUATE INSTRUCTIONAL MATERIALS?

William H. Durr

UPTODATE school programs require a wide variety of instructional materials geared to the interests and abilities of children. These materials include motion pictures, slides, filmstrips, recordings, radio, and television—in addition to books, maps and charts.

The following list of questions has been prepared so that you can determine the adequacy of your school's instructional materials. A study of the questions you checked as "no" will point up areas which may need improvement.

Reprinted from
JOURNAL OF THE NATIONAL EDUCATION ASSOCIATION

YES   NO

Administration

1. Does your school system have a director of audio-visual education or instructional materials?
2. Does this person perform the following services?
   [a] Supervise selection of materials for purchase and addition to your audio-visual department.
   [b] Inform teachers about available materials.
   [c] Assist in providing audio-visual facilities.
   [d] Provide for the distribution of materials to teachers when needed.
   [e] Help teachers to make good use of materials.
3. Is there a person in your building who serves as coordinator of audio-visual instruction?
4. Does he have released time from teaching to carry thru these responsibilties?
5. Are any of the teachers active members of
   [a] NEA Department of Audio-visual Instruction?
   [b] State or local audio-visual organizations?
6. Is there an advisory committee on audio-visual instruction in your school system, with members of the teaching staff on the committee?
7. Does this committee assist in formulating plans and policy for the development and operation of the audio-visual program in your schools?
8. Do teachers assist in the selection of instructional materials for purchase for your school?

Materials

9. Do teachers in your school have readily available the following types of materials?
    - Motion pictures
    - Filmstrips
    - Slides
    - Recordings
    - Flat pictures
    - Maps and charts
    - Models and exhibit materials

           YES   **NO**

10. Does the budget permit teachers to rent and pay postage on materials such as films which they need to use in their instruction and which are not available locally?
11. Does your school provide equipment and materials that teachers and pupils may use in producing their own audio-visual materials, such as cameras, film, slide-making materials, recorders, mounting board?

Information on Materials

12. Is there information on local resources which may be used on field trips or at school?
13. Do teachers have ready access to catalogs and listings of available materials?
14. Are materials frequently displayed so that teachers become aware of them and are encouraged to use them?
15. Are teachers invited to frequent the audio-visual center to browse and find out what materials are available?

Distribution of Materials

16. Is it easy for teachers to request the use of audio-visual materials?
17. Are teachers informed in advance whether requested materials will be delivered to them when needed?
18. Are such materials provided to teachers for sufficient periods of time to permit preview, proper showing, and re-showing?
19. Does the center provide for keeping materials and equipment in good condition?

Facilities for Using Materials

20. Can the amount of light in the classrooms be controlled so that films can be projected clearly?
21. Are there electrical outlets in the front and back of each room?
22. Is the following equipment available?
    - Sound motion-picture projector
    - Filmstrip and slide projector
    - Three-speed record and transcription player
    - Tape recorder
    - Radio
    - Television receiver
    - Opaque projector
    - Overhead projector

Facilities for Using Materials (*Continued*)

	YES	NO
23. Do classrooms have adequate bulletinboard space?	___	___
24. Are there rails or racks in classrooms to permit display of maps, charts, etc.?	___	___
25. Is there space provided for convenient storage of equipment when it is not in use?	___	___
26. Is there space for storage of materials which is open to teachers so that they can readily and easily check on materials that are available?	___	___
27. Are there facilities and materials that will permit teachers and pupils to prepare photographic pictures, handmade lantern slides, mounted flat pictures, etc., for class use?	___	___

Utilization of Materials

28. Have most teachers had courses in audio-visual instruction?
29. Do most teachers make regular use of motion pictures, slides, filmstrips, and recordings as an integral part of their classroom instruction?
30. Can all teachers operate the audio-visual equipment available?
31. Do teachers make use of field trips as an aid to developing better pupil understanding?
32. Do teachers make it a practice to preview materials before using them with a class?
33. Do teachers help pupils establish objectives for seeing the film before it is shown?
34. Do teachers frequently re-show materials when they feel that such re-showing will materially aid pupil learning?
35. Are audio-visual materials used in faculty meetings or by teacher study groups?
36. Are audio-visual materials used in PTA meetings or with other out-of-school groups to interpret the school program?
37. Are there books and magazines dealing with audio-visual instruction in your school's professional library?
38. Does your school have students trained to assist with the operation of audio-visual equipment?

OTHER PUBLICATIONS

DEPARTMENT OF AUDIO-VISUAL INSTRUCTION
NATIONAL EDUCATION ASSOCIATION OF THE UNITED STATES
1201 Sixteenth Street, N.W., Washington 6, D.C.

Planning Schools for Use of Audio-Visual Materials — No. 1 Classrooms
Price, $1.00

Planning Schools for Use of Audio-Visual Materials — No. 2 Auditoriums
Price, $1.00

Audio-Visual COMMUNICATION REVIEW
A professional and research quarterly
Subscription, $4.00

Guide to Films in Economic Education
Price, $1.00

Conference Proceedings 1952
Price, $0.75

Conference Proceedings 1953
Price, $0.75

All publications, except Audio-Visual COMMUNICATION REVIEW, are subject to the following discounts on quality orders:

2 to 9 copies	10%
10 to 99 copies	25%
100 or more	33 1/3%

Orders for $1.00 or less must be accompanied by a check or money order.

www.ingramcontent.com/pod-product-compliance
Lightning Source LLC
Chambersburg PA
CBHW051104230426
43667CB00013B/2435